End

MW01013137

Emma Stark is a refreshing voice among the modern-day prophets, and that voice comes through loud and clear in *The Prophetic Warrior*. In this timely book, Emma uses her bold, redemptive truth-telling style, along with her smart humor, to bring forth a message so vital to the church in this hour. She not only calls for the prophetic warriors to arise, she equips them with inspiring examples and practical keys to walk in faith, war in the spirit, and prophesy with accuracy. Every prophetic person needs to read this book!

—Jennifer LeClaire
Founder of Awakening House of Prayer
Author of *The Making of a Prophet*

In *The Prophetic Warrior* Emma Stark gives us a powerful and thought-provoking look at how the prophetic should function in the life of every believer. Regardless of how long you have operated in hearing the voice of the Lord, you will be challenged to move into a greater level of authority and make Jesus real everywhere you go!

—Jane Hamon
Co-Apostle, Vision Church @ Christian International
Author of *Dreams and Visions, The Deborah Company,
The Cyrus Decree, Discernment*

The Church in Western society looks nothing like the Spirit-empowered people that the risen and ascended Jesus has commissioned to bring His heavenly Kingdom on earth and bring His return. The vision of a miraculous Christian life and the significance of prophetic ministry described in this book are what God is restoring to His Church. *The Prophetic Warrior* is a word for our time that not only reveals the transformation God is calling us to, but also equips us to step into it. Emma Stark lives what she writes, as the great Kingdom stories in this book show. Reading it will release faith in you, teach you how to exercise your authority in prayer, and guide you in how to grow in your God-given gifting and calling.

—Rev. Canon John McGinley
Vicar, Holy Trinity Church Leicester, England
Head of Church Planting Development, New Wine

It is with great pleasure that I endorse this dynamic message and book. In *The Prophetic Warrior*, Emma has provided an exceptional message that will awaken, activate, and commission the gift of prophecy and the confidence to stand as a victorious warrior. You will be empowered in faith to be an abandoned and bold prophetic warrior to see His Kingdom purposes birthed, lives radically touched and transformed. You will learn how to walk and function in the supernatural in a way that will captivate the lost, bring salvation, strike fear into the ranks of darkness, bring healing and resurrection life. If you desire to be used of the Lord, to prophesy accurate life-transforming words, and to defeat schemes of darkness, this book is a must-read. Thank you, Emma, for this fresh, inspiring, and transformational message. It is a now word and one of the best teachings on prophecy being released in this time.

—Rebecca Greenwood
Christian Harvest International
Strategic Prayer Apostolic Network
Author of *Authority to Tread, Destined to Rule, Let Our Children Go,
Defeating Strongholds of the Mind, Glory Warfare*

Emma Stark lives this book, and that means she has something to impart into us. We live in a powerful time! What God is saying and doing in Heaven must be manifested on earth. In this book Emma challenges and equips us to a new level of courage, faith, and authority to manifest God's will. I have always believed prophets are warriors who set captives free. Every time we prophesy something should change!

Emma dares us to deal with our fear of the enemy and believe the Kingdom of God is not an equal and opposite opposing force to the kingdom of darkness. There is no equal between us and the devil! So it is our responsibility to stir up the gifts God has given us and to open our spiritual eyes to see new territory God has for us. Remembering that we, the Church, are the determining factor for what happens in the nations.

—Dr. Sharon Stone
Founder of Christian International Europe

This book is brilliant! It will make you thoroughly uncomfortable with where you are in your experience with God. It will challenge you to be more courageous and to push your boundaries to see people and nations set free by the power of the prophetic word that He uses you to give. Well done to Emma Stark for writing this valuable field manual for a new generation of prophets and prophetic people who are determined to see change come and Jesus's name lifted high in our lifetimes!

—Dr. Arleen Westerhof
Founder, Netherlands Prophetic Council
Co-Senior Leader, God's Embassy Amsterdam
Author of IMPACT: *Prophesy and Change the World*

Emma Stark has inspired so many of us through her exceptional prophetic gift and has dedicated herself to raising up others in prophetic ministry. In her new book, *The Prophetic Warrior*, Emma encourages, provokes, and motivates us to discover what a prophetic culture looks like for each one of us. In this three-part book, we are taken on a journey of testimonies and teaching through faith, war, and prophecy to discover who we are, what we carry, and how we can live a prophetic lifestyle. This practical and inspiring book includes activations and declarations to put into practice what you have just read. Put this book to good use as it's packed with application and real-life examples. You will not be disappointed.

—Tim Eldridge
Co-Director, Presence Ministries International and
European Leaders Alliance

One of the things I have declared about this new decade is that there is a fresh prophetic move being birthed. Not only is there a fresh move, but there are fresh ways of releasing God's prophetic heart to individuals as well as regions and nations, including their leaders. Emma Stark has captured in words what I have declared. I love this book and the freshness with which she expresses both the identity and function of the prophetic warrior. This book is fresh, relevant to the new generation arising and challenging. Furthermore, I found this book fun and engaging. It is the NEW!

—Barbara J. Yoder
Lead Apostle, Shekinah Regional Apostolic Center
Breakthrough Apostolic Ministries Network

This is a book that will challenge you to find your God-given voice and then speak confidently. With intellectual and biblical depth, great illustrations and practical truths, this book will shape your understanding of the prophetic gift and help you discover your sound.

—Rachel Hickson
Founder and Director, Heartcry for Change

Through incredible stories that will challenge your faith, Emma Stark has made an amazing resource available to the body of Christ in this book. If you are looking to be equipped, inspired, and activated in the prophetic, this book is for you!

—James Aladiran
Founder, Prayer Storm

THE
Prophetic Warrior

THE
Prophetic
Warrior

OPERATING IN YOUR TRUE
PROPHETIC AUTHORITY

EMMA STARK

DESTINY IMAGE® PUBLISHERS, INC.
P.O. Box 310, Shippensburg, PA 17257-0310
"Promoting Inspired Lives."

This book and all other Destiny Image and Destiny Image Fiction books are available at Christian bookstores and distributors worldwide.

For more information on foreign distributors, call 717-532-3040.

Or reach us on the Internet: www.destinyimage.com

ISBN 13 TP: 978-0-7684-5171-9

ISBN 13 Ebook: 978-0-7684-5172-6

HC ISBN: 978-0-7684-5174-0

LP ISBN: 978-0-7684-5173-3

Cover design by Eileen Rockwell

Interior design by Jeffrey M. Hall

For Worldwide Distribution, Printed in the U.S.A.

3 4 5 6 7 8 9 10 11 / 24 23 22 21 20

Dedication

This book is dedicated to

My husband, David, the most intelligent, handsome, remarkable, and godly man I know. Your love and patience, wisdom and devotion knows no bounds. I am the most blessed woman to have you.

My children—Jessica, Peter and Samuel, you are my joy and delight. Your adventurous wild hearts and beautiful faces cheer me on. You are wonderful, and I thank God that He gave us to each other. You are the place my heart is most alive!

My parents, John and Liz Hansford, who taught me to love Jesus and His Church; your truth and wisdom have been the ever-present anchor in my life.

Sarah-Jane Biggart, my dearest friend—you are beautiful. Your support and adventuring companionship is one of God's greatest gifts to me.

Acknowledgements

This book has been in gestation for many years, and I am grateful to all those prophetic voices who called it into being and encouraged me to write down the stories and teachings that have been shared on a microphone many times over the last decade. In particular, Cindy Jacobs, who stood me up in front of hundreds of people to say, basically, "God says hurry up and write the book!" Cindy, the archetypal prophetic warrior, has blazed a trail for prophets, male and female. Thank you for making a space for this bold Irish woman amongst the global prophetic community where I have found so many mothers and fathers, running mates and fellow warriors.

Of course, after receiving prophetic words, we then have to "fight the good fight." Larry Sparks and Tina Pugh of Destiny Image have made this part of the process a genuinely good fight through their remarkable and constant encouragement and championing of me and my efforts.

Dr. Sharon Stone, my mother in the prophetic—you have been the pioneer for prophets and prophecy in the British Isles and Europe, and we are honored to stand on your shoulders. Thank you for battling through to make a way for the rest of us.

Everyone tells me, "You sound like a CI (Christian International) prophet," and this is a proud badge to wear. Thank you, Bishop Bill, Tom, Jane and all the Hamons, and Christian International network. I know that there is probably a lot of the sound of all of you in this book.

So many hundreds of individuals and families, some known to us personally but many unknown, have supported David and me and our ministry since we stepped out in faith to build a global prophetic community from a small base in Scotland. Words are not enough to express our gratitude for your generosity and partnership.

Last but not least, to everyone in the Glasgow Prophetic Centre/ Global Prophetic Alliance "forever family": truly this book belongs to each one of you. Prophecy is a team activity, and you have made it all a joy and a delight. Thank you!

Contents

By Cindy Jacobs

You are about to read an incredible book by an amazing woman of God. As I read the following pages, I immediately thought, "This message is so timely!" My second thought was, "Emma Stark has a style of writing that speaks right to your heart."

Let me explain. Emma is real and authentic. This book will provoke you to greater things while feeling that you are being mentored by her personally. It is sad that I read it instead of listening in an audible form because she is absolutely powerful and delightful when she speaks.

Chapter 1 jumps right in with the title "Weaponized by Heaven." She makes Heaven so real for us. Her statement "How big must the robe of God be to fill the space where 100 million angels are in perpetual worship" gives you a glimpse of what I mean.

I read those words and just had a sweet moment with God. She makes the point that God has given us gifts right from the throne room of Heaven.

Her crystal-clear message that we are equipped by God to use the gift of prophecy to set many free is both wonderful and challenging! We need to sharpen our ability to hear God and share it with others. Her statement that sometimes we need a "fire and a hammer" word to break down strongholds that have been up in people's lives is so accurate.

I remember one time giving a word over the grandson of a friend. The word was simple, "You are not stupid. In fact, you are very smart." I had no idea that his ten-year-old self struggled with feeling inadequate in the area of brains! From that day on he changed his mindset and became a successful student.

That memory made me think that you might be feeling rather ignorant and not talented in the realm of flowing in spiritual gifts. Emma has written a book that will help you correct that thinking and awaken in the area of flowing with a warrior spirit to help liberate others through God's power.

I find that one of the least understood abilities that God has bestowed upon us is to use the authority He has given us to annihilate satan's inroads into our lives. We are not called to live deflated lives; we are to be overcomers!

Get ready to have a great adventure with God as you read *The Prophetic Warrior*! You will be changed!

—Cindy Jacobs
Generals International
Dallas, Texas

By Dr. James W. Goll

I tend to act as a scout in the Holy Spirit, surveying the landscape. I always have my spiritual antennas out, my eyes and ears open for the Holy Spirit to reveal to me "voices that need to be heard." I am on the lookout for consecrated believers in the Lord Jesus Christ who are carrying a distinct sound—a new sound—a fresh anointing.

Like a Samuel, I am peering into the heart of a matter and asking the Holy Spirit to show me new dread champions for the prophetic cause of Christ. These are those who are not just repackaging the same ole thing in another new wrapping paper, but who are fresh themselves and deliver their "now word" with relevancy to a hungry church into a broken world.

I call these chosen vessels "treasure chests." Matthew 13:52 states, *"And Jesus said to them, 'Therefore every scribe who has become a disciple of the kingdom of heaven is like a head of a household, who brings out of his treasure things new and old'"* (NASB). We are each called be treasure chests for the Kingdom of God who store up and bring forth treasures both *"new and old."* But did you notice the order? Treasures both *"new and old."* So, we must be people who honor our rich church history and those who labored diligently before us, but we must also be a steward of the "fresh, now word" so desperately needed.

Consecrated Carriers

Some carry a word for a moment, but a moment only. They might carry a "now word" but in reality, it has no long-term effect. They can tend to be a part of the flavor of the month club in the sometimes fickle Body of Christ. They appear on the scene with a flash and a splash, and then they disappear or fall in front of everyone's eyes as quickly as they appeared, because they did not have the character necessary to carry the content. So, then if it is more than simply the next rising star, then what am I on the lookout for then?

As veteran of full-time vocational ministry for over forty-five years, and as a survivor and thriver of multiple moves of the Holy Spirit, my heart pounds within me when I find the prophetic potential of five key components: 1) consecration, 2) content, 3) charisma, 4) character, and most importantly, 5) Christos. What did you say? We hear a lot about the fivefold ministry gifts, but what about the fivefold in the context of the five c's? There we go!

God is looking for those who are, number one, consecrated and set apart unto Him and not superficially glitzy like the world. And does the Word of God matter? Oh yes, it does! These are those who have the second element called content. This comes from reading, devouring, and praying the Word of God. It oozes out of their very pores.

Another key component is charisma. Are they anointed by the Holy Spirit? With these servant leaders, the gifts of God are freely flowing, and there is a supernatural dimension to their lives. And what about character? If the gifts cannot be earned and they are a trademark of the amazing grace of God, then is there a flip side to this thing called discipleship? Charisma is God's free gift to us and others, but character is our gift back to our heavenly Father and then to those around us. Yes, character matters!

What is this Christos thing you are referring to? Does the person live for Jesus? Do they walk with Jesus? Do they teach others how to be like Jesus? The true spirit of prophecy is the testimony of Jesus! Is Christ the center of who they are, what they teach, and how they live? If so, I am on board! When the five c's meet the fivefold, we have consecrated carriers!

The Compassion of God

As I compose these words for the foreword of the consecrated, courageous prophetic warrior Emma Stark, I am weeping out of gratitude that I get to see the next generation arising who exhibit exactly what I am talking about. They are a new breed of compassionate warriors for Christ Jesus, who live their lives on their knees and then get up and run to the battle. Oh, this elates this once young, zealous man who is now older and a veteran! This is what makes Papa God and Jesus's heart skip a beat! A generation of prophetic warriors is here!

You are holding in your hand old truths made new. You are holding in your hands a needed arsenal to equip and train the Body of Christ to be all they can be in Christ Jesus. You are holding in your hands a stick of explosive dynamite! It is indeed my honor to commend to you the life, the teachings, and the anointing that rests upon one of God's chosen ones for such a time as this! Great job, Emma!

Read this. Eat this. Become the content in this book!

With Gratitude,

—Dr. James W. Goll
Founder of God Encounters Ministries
GOLL Ideation LLC

Introduction

Why on earth have they invited me here?" I wondered as I stood up to minister in a church that I'd never been to before. The people didn't look in any way open to the Holy Spirit; they had never had a visit from a prophet, and all in all, they looked very displeased to see me there! I sighed internally and made a mental note to check my invitations more fully before accepting them in the future. Forcing a smile, I took the microphone and quietly asked God: "Would you please give me a 'killer' prophetic word, so that I can try to get us all working together here?"

God replied, "Yes. Go and publicly deal with that young lady's infertility."

"No, Lord, that is not a great idea! Can I have another word please?"

"No," He said, "just deal with her first."

I was aware of the awkward silence in the room as I wrestled some more with God.

As I walked toward the young woman, the very first words that church ever heard a prophet say were, "I would like to deal with your infertility. Oh, hang on, God has just said that it's not you, it's your husband. Is he here?"

Her husband wasn't present, and the shocked, concerned, sharp intake of breath from everyone was clearly audible.

God then told me to pray very specifically, and so I turned to face the congregation and said, "I am sorry if this offends you. I am going to pray something very fast, so that you can forget it if you don't like it. God has said to this woman that 'you will conceive and bear children if I bless your husband's sperm.' So I bless his sperm to be 'commando,' in Jesus's name."

At this the church pastor jumped to his feet and grabbed the microphone from my hand. I think I'm about to be marched out!

But instead he began to weep and said, "The young man who you are praying for is my son. He has had years of treatment for leukemia and was finally discharged from the hospital last week. Our final question to the consultant was, 'Will he ever have children?' We prayed for a sign that we would be grandparents, and you have answered all our prayers."

From that moment on the whole service took a radical upturn!

This book is a journey into the thinking and lifestyle of a prophetic warrior. In it you will learn the importance of courage, faith, and understanding your true authority. It is an open invitation for you to find your wild revelatory voice and to become established in who you were meant to be.

THE GREATER WORKS

I grew up on the rural north coast of Ireland. My father was an Irish Baptist minister; he was hardworking and full of wisdom. We were traditional spiritually, and broadly cessationalist: we knew the Holy Spirit in a non-relational way.

But our hearts were burning for more.

I didn't know about "tongues" until I left home at eighteen. I'd never really seen a healing miracle, and I certainly had no grid *at all* for prophecy, deliverance, or spiritual warfare. However, I had seen "in the spirit" ever since I could remember (although back then I didn't know what it was called). I saw faces of angels and demons and had no understanding what they were. I had "premonitions," with no useful language to express them.

I did have the Word of God in huge quantities; I memorized large sections of Scripture for Sunday school prize competitions. One verse above all gripped me in those early years, and still does today:

> *Very truly I tell you, whoever believes in me will do the works I have been doing, and they will do even greater works than these, because I am going to the Father* (John 14:12).

I remember being in the car one Sunday night, driving with my dad to hear him preach and asking him, "Why doesn't your church do the greater works of Jesus? In fact, why doesn't your church do the basic works of Jesus? I don't think we are a very 'biblically normal' church!"

Jesus walks through walls and floats in the sky and talks to two dead men. He walks on water, messes up every funeral He goes to, and heals people all the time!

My teenage heart longed for biblical authenticity; I was biblically curious.

What does it mean to do the "greater works"? These are clearly not more *significant* than what Jesus did. *Greater* means mega, larger, mighty, huge. It also means surprising, abundant, and complete.[1]

It is therefore not a stretch to say we will do things that show the fullness of God. He has more to pour out than could be seen in Jesus's three years of ministry—surprising things that demonstrate abundance. We have moved into a time when miracles, signs, and wonders are marrying the prophetic, and a new breed of revelatory people is emerging. Expect the *fullness* of God to work through *you*. Expect it to look strange. Expect it in *your* life and *your family's* life. Expect to see miracles that you have not seen before. God will speak in new and strange ways!

We already see the progress of "greater works" in Acts. The woman with the issue of blood had to walk and bend down to touch Jesus's garment in order to be healed (see Luke 8:43–48). But the *greater work* came with Paul, when his garments were sent out to heal the sick—people didn't even need to go to him (see Acts 19:11–12). This is a work of fullness and multiplication. It develops further again with Peter, whose shadow healed, with no clothes involved (see Acts 5:15)! The power of God oozed out of the disciples, indicating fullness.

YOU ARE IN ERROR

Jesus speaks with His usual, razor-sharp insight in Matthew 22:29:

You are in error because you do not know the Scriptures or the power of God.

Not one of us wants to see Jesus point a finger and call us out for being in error!

Are *we* in error because we don't know the Scriptures or the power of God?

What does it look like to be in error because *you do not know the Scriptures?*

You would be full of heresy. It's a church that would redefine marriage, a church that would not worry about sex before marriage, a church that would appoint actively homosexual clergy. It's a church with no focus on holiness or on anything uncomfortable.

What does it look like to be in error because *you do not know the power of God?*

It would be a church full of religion and over-systemized to make things work. It would be a church busy in do-gooding, where all man power and money power is sunk into well-meaning social action projects that focus on justice and kindness in a community (which are still important), but with no expectation or demonstration of miraculous healings, hearing from God, prophecy, lives changed, or deliverance from the bondage of demons. Its focus would be schemes of fun church, café church, or church programs that are well branded to look modern but that have no underpinning or needing of the Holy Spirit to function. A. W. Tozer wrote:

> If the Holy Spirit was withdrawn from the church today, ninety-five percent of what we do would go on and no-one would know the difference. If the Holy Spirit had been withdrawn from the New Testament church,

ninety-five percent of what they did would stop, and everybody would know the difference.[2]

Today it is *not* business as usual in the Body of Christ. It is *not* same old, same old. The *power* of God will be seen like never before. We only have a toe in the water of what God is about to do in us, through us, and for us! There is a burning revelation that is boiling inside of me and it is that God says, *"My power will be seen in the nations."*

If we were to summate this current time in the earth, it would be in three words: *new means new!*

Truly we have not been this way before. Everything will look different—leaders, structures, educations systems, financial systems, church buildings, and how we operate. God has hit the reset button. It is foolishness to expect the old things to remain, to think that the old things will work. God will give us a *"vomiting anointing"* that we might spit out what will no longer carry Him in this time, and just as God threw up the Laodiceans in Revelation 3, so we also will join Him in getting rid of that which does not reflect Him.

I am not prophesying that one day you will walk in the new; *you are in the new right now!* Our hearts must cry out, *"I'd rather be an amateur in the new than an expert in the old!"*

It is time to break agreement with smallness and the shrunken ways that you have thought in the past. It is time to break with repetitive thinking, for God is releasing a new mindset to you. You will receive new thoughts, new plans, new ideas, new creativity, and fresh anointings, and you will have prophecy that flows from you.

You will be *living in the river* of revelation, not dipping in and out, not warming yourself up. You will be so in the presence of God as a lifestyle that you will prophesy at length with the windows of

Heaven open and the downloads will pour over you! Those who have been nervous about the prophetic and have never prophesied will overflow with revelation.

There will be a rush of people who will flow with prophetic revelation. You will lose your fear of being a bold truth-teller. You will break out of the fear of your own voice, and you will break out of the fear of failure.

The stifling of the prophetic will be no more, and you will prophesy like never before, receiving revelatory upgrades. Words of knowledge and power that bring life will come forth. Your voice will command the impossible to come to pass. Your mouth will become a house of intense revelation. Your mouth will become a house of creation; there is a new anointing to *create* what has not been seen before.

This is a time when you will be going *beyond* where you have been before. You will go *beyond* where you have gone in provision and seeing God move in your finances.

You will go *beyond*:

- your last war and victory
- your last level of strength
- your last level of glory
- your last business deal
- your last level of working miracles, signs, and wonders
- where the Church has been
- even your wildest expectations and dreams

It is a time to step over and step into the days of *going beyond*, for this is the epoch where the *prophetic warriors* will arise, and God's words will rest in their mouths, and they will call into order what is in disarray.

And the Lord welcomes you into all this right now.

PART I

FAITH

CHAPTER 1

Weaponized by Heaven

Spread out above the heads of the living creatures was what looked something like a vault, sparkling like crystal, and awesome. Under the vault their wings were stretched out one toward the other, and each had two wings covering its body. When the creatures moved, I heard the sound of their wings, like the roar of rushing waters, like the voice of the Almighty, like the tumult of an army. When they stood still, they lowered their wings. Then there came a voice from above the vault over their heads as they stood with lowered wings. Above the vault over their heads was what looked like a throne of lapis lazuli, and high above on the throne was a figure like that of a man. I saw that from what appeared to be his waist up he looked like glowing metal, as if full of fire, and that from there down he looked like fire; and brilliant light surrounded him. Like the appearance of a rainbow in the clouds on a rainy day, so was the radiance around him. This was the appearance of the likeness of the glory of the LORD. When I saw it, I fell facedown, and I heard the voice of one speaking.

—Ezekiel 1:22–28

WHERE DOES PROPHECY COME FROM?

Have you ever wondered what Heaven and the New Jerusalem are really like?

Have you wondered what smells would invade you or what sights would dazzle you as you walked along Heaven's main street?

Have you ever been caught up by Jesus into the heavenly realms and seen it for yourself, like Ezekiel was?

Let's delve straight into Scripture to find out how Heaven is described to us. Moses, Ezekiel, and John give us great insight into the heavenly daily life and rhythms.[3] They tell us that there are streets of gold that are simultaneously as clear as crystal. The walls are gloriously translucent, made of jasper; Heaven's foundations are precious stones, and there is a river of life running through it, flowing from the throne of God. There are trees lining Heaven's central avenue that are incredibly producing twelve different kinds of fruit and are so bursting with life that their harvests need to be reaped every *month*![4]

I often wonder who is assigned to collect the fruit from these heavenly trees? What recipes do they create from these amazing harvests? What dishes will make up the wedding feast at the marriage of the Lamb? I love to think of angels working away in the heavenly kitchens and poring over the perfect menus for this banquet!

Have you ever been caught up by Jesus
into the heavenly realms and seen it
for yourself, like Ezekiel was?

But beyond any doubt, the most important place in all of Heaven is the place where God's throne resides.

THE THRONE ROOM OF HEAVEN

The Bible tell us that the throne room of Heaven is a *very* full place! Around its outside edge are many angels. We are given a math sum in Revelation 5 to help us number the angels in the throne room alone: *"ten thousand times ten thousand."* That's 100 million angels.

So if you started walking toward the middle of the throne room from one edge, you may well get lost in this angel crowd, and it would probably take at least a few days to traverse the throne room floor!

The deafening noise of the angels' devoted song of worship would fill your ears: 100 million voices proclaiming, *"Worthy is the Lamb!"* They are singing with one resounding roar to God on the throne and to the Lamb, Jesus Christ. They are proclaiming how *different* He is from anyone or anything else who has ever been or ever will be; how powerful, wealthy, wise, and strong He is; how breathtakingly glorious and beautiful He is.[5]

Finally, upon reaching the center of this noisy and full arena, you would find the living creatures and the elders encircling the very throne. There are twenty-four thrones, with twenty-four elders sitting on them, each wearing crowns of gold but eagerly casting them down at God's feet.

The four living creatures each have six wings and eyes all over their bodies. (My children have often asked me, with incredulity, questions like, "Do they even have eyes in their armpits?," "What does 'eyes all over' look like?,", "Can you make me a costume to look like a living creature?")

If you were then to raise your gaze over the tops of the heads of these incredible creatures, you would see a huge throne above, with someone *practically indescribable* seated on it.

You would see our Lord God Almighty on the throne, with the appearance of jasper, ruby, and carnelian, and very bright, glowing hot metal. In other words, God is shining resplendent with fiery red and orange colors! A full rainbow that looks like an emerald is encircling His throne.

This throne is deep blue sapphire, flaming with fire, and its wheels are all ablaze. The throne's foundations are righteousness and justice. The train of God's robe fills the whole temple.

How big must the robe of God be to fill the space where 100 million angels are in perpetual worship?

There are clouds around Him, lit up by flashing lightning and explosions of brilliant light. A volcanic river of fire is flowing out from before Him.

In front of the throne there is what looks like a sea of glass, clear as crystal. There are seven flaming lamps. And as if the roar of Heaven's voices was not deafening enough, out of the throne is coming awesome rumblings and thundering.

You are now in the very throne room of God, the heart of Heaven.

How big must the robe of God be to fill the space where 100 million angels are in perpetual worship?

Ascension Day

Meanwhile, picture the scene down here on Earth, on a mountaintop outside Jerusalem in first-century Judea.

It is Ascension Day, the day Jesus's body left the earthly realm, and this remarkable Jewish man (who has risen from the grave) is enveloped in a chariot cloud that transports Him to the Father. At this very moment in history, Jesus Christ, the Son of God, the Risen Lamb, walks back into the throne room of Heaven!

His eyes are burning with fire; His hair is as white as wool; *"His voice as the sound of many waters"* (Rev. 1:15 NKJV). He sounds more remarkable than the cascades of water at Niagara Falls. His feet are glowing, as though they were in a blacksmith's furnace. He has a golden sash on His robe, and coming out of His mouth is a sharp, double-edged sword. His face is like the sun shining in all its brilliance.

This is the ascension moment, a moment of enthroning Jesus.

This is His reentry into Heaven. He moves to take His place at the right hand of the Father, and in a statement of permanence, He sits down.

He has come home. He has returned. He is not bound to the earthly realm anymore.

He has *ascended to the throne room, and all authority and power is His.*

> [Jesus is] *far above all rule and authority, power and dominion, and every name that is invoked, not only in the present age but also in the one to come. And God placed all things under his feet and appointed him to be head over everything* (Ephesians 1:21–22).

Jesus's throne in Heaven marginalizes all earthly thrones. Every other throne or king is puny in comparison. His rule has supremacy over all other thrones, principalities, and powers. Nothing compares to His power and splendor.

Then the most remarkable thing happens!

Jesus's attention turns to us, and one of the first things He does in this new, ascended place is to give us gifts:

> *When he ascended on high, he took many captives and gave gifts to his people* (Ephesians 4:8).

Who are the captives mentioned in this verse? Matthew 27 delightfully (and shockingly) writes of many holy people who had died coming back to life at the same time as Jesus. They also went visiting people in Jerusalem, appearing to many. These people fly with Jesus, back to the throne room. What a celebration it must have been when God the Father received Jesus and the captives back home!

> ### *One of the first things that Jesus does in His new, ascended place is to give us gifts.*

We are handed gifts!

In the very midst of these festivities of receiving Jesus the conquering King, at the point of ascension, we are handed gifts! One of those gifts is prophecy; other gifts include miraculous powers, healing, tongues, faith, discerning of spirits, words of knowledge, words of wisdom, interpretation of tongues, prophets, apostles, evangelists, teachers, and shepherds.

By the way, it is worth remembering that there is a gift called "miraculous powers." Perhaps it is the most forgotten in the 1 Corinthians 12 list of gifts, but Jesus walked on water, walked through walls, floated in the air, shone resplendent in glory at the transfiguration, disturbed funerals by raising the dead, changed the weather, and we too are handed the ability for miraculous powers!

- Miraculous powers sees Joshua command the sun to stand still.
- Miraculous powers enables Moses to see water pour from a rock.
- Miraculous power is attached to Jehoshaphat's worship, and his enemies end up killing each other before God's people even turn up!
- Miraculous power sees the Red Sea part, opening a way where there seemed to be no way.

Is this a gift that you have asked for?

Is miraculous powers a gift that you have asked for?

Throne room gifts to enforce the Kingdom

All these gifts come from the most powerful place in all the heavenly and earthly realms and are given to us so that we might *enforce* the Kingdom of Jesus Christ. As we partner with the Holy Spirit and use these gifts, we become directors of Heaven on earth; we are trusted ambassadors who can legislate for His Kingdom with each use of every gift.

And perhaps one of Jesus's first thoughts when He returned to Heaven with the captives was, "How am I going to *weaponize* My people with My power?" He would have been considering the abundance of what He needed us to have to make us unstoppable and to empower us without limit to change the world! Remember, Jesus is not mean or stingy, and He doesn't hold back from giving us the very best.

Prophecy, healing, tongues, and *miraculous powers* are not "optional extras" that we can take or leave, depending on what mood we wake up in.

> **Prophecy, healing, tongues and miraculous powers are not "optional extras" that we can take or leave, depending on what mood we wake up in.**

WEAPONIZED BY HEAVEN

Spiritual gifts

For years we have yo-yoed with our focus on spiritual gifts, struggling at times to see their relevance and often not seeing them as necessities for everyday life.

One of the problems we have in seeing gifts as fundamentally important is with our translation of the Greek word *charisma* (translated "gift") that Paul writes about to the church in Corinth.

> *There are different kinds of gifts, but the same Spirit distributes them* (1 Corinthians 12:4).

We see the word *gift* and think of fun, frivolous, and not particularly useful like a quirky and strange Christmas gift given by an elderly and out-of-touch relative!

Yet *charisma* means spiritual enablement or spiritual empowerments; spiritual endowment; given free, in undeserved favor. In fact, the root meaning of the word *charisma* means to rescue.[6]

Spiritual gifts are extraordinary powers, given liberally and without us earning them. They are for *all* believers, no matter what you think of yourself. This means you must lay down and release your hold on any low self-esteem and self-rejection still operational in you right now.

Spiritual gifts are empowerments provided by God to manifest His Kingdom and to rescue others. You have been weaponized by Heaven! This truth must underpin our attitude to them.

You have been weaponized by Heaven!

The gifts are not optional, extra additions for our lives or only for a few special people. Prophecy, healing, tongues, words of knowledge, words of wisdom, and discerning of spirits are gifts in the same way that bagpipes, tartans, swords, haggis, and the *cèilidh* dance are gifts to the Scottish people! It is *who* the Scottish are; they're intrinsic to their identity. Think Scotland, think tartan. Think spiritual gifts and powerful miracles, think the Church—think *you*!

Divine empowerments

When we read of the coming of the Holy Spirit, it is expressed in a very determined way:

> *But you shall receive* power *when the Holy Spirit has come upon you* (Acts 1:8 NKJV).

The Greek word for power is *dunamis,* but one of this word's first meanings is "force." In other words, one might say, "You will receive a *force* when the Holy Spirit comes upon you!"

When you use spiritual gifts, you have remarkable ability, explosive strength, and forceful power!

Likewise, we read: *"The kingdom of God is not in word but in **power** "* (1 Cor. 4:20 NKJV).

"Power" here also means "force." The Kingdom of God is not in word but is a spiritual force.

It is time for it to dawn on us *just how far we have fallen* from the original intent of God to make us a spiritual force, with military capabilities and the power to rescue people.

We are usually more interested in being well thought of, or not wanting to stand out too much, or of avoiding being too strange or different. We are often too afraid to step toward others in fear that we might accidentally offend them.

We have surrendered and lost the mindset of *power* and the thought process that, "I have been asked to intervene in the world and to rescue many."

We must recapture an inner way of seeing the world that understands that "I am a solution; I am carrying spiritual nuclear bombs and prophetic flamethrowers! My spiritual slingshot, my gift of prophecy, my bow and arrow, my gift of healing, will liberate you and show you Jesus!"

The spiritual gifts are divine empowerments to operate in the power of God to rescue people.

CHAPTER 2

What Do the Gifts Look Like in Real Life?

It's never too late to be what you might have been.

—**Attributed to George Eliot, Novelist**

THE PREGNANT SHOP ASSISTANT

I love to shop for shoes. I love to go shoe shopping with God, hearing what He thinks about colors, for example. In our shopping conversations I might ask God questions like why He made red (a personal favorite of mine), what He likes about red, what the color communicates when it's used in art, what it heals when painted on a wall, or how He speaks through the color when it's worn as clothing.

One day I was clutching what were soon-to-be the newest additions to my collection of red, high heels, and I was walking toward the checkout line to pay for them. As I did so, God said to me, "I like those shoes in your hand. I sometimes wear red shoes. Now, go prophesy over the young girl at the cash register."

At that very moment, a divinely orchestrated series of events began to occur: the line suddenly disappeared, and all the checkout operators—except one—instantly shut their registers and left the payment area. God had completely set things up to the point that the only people anywhere around were me and the young girl He had told me to prophesy to.

I set my shoes down on the counter in front of her and said, "Hi, I'm Emma. I'm a prophet who hears from God."

The young woman looked stunned. This is a normal response when I'm introducing myself, but if you don't tell people what you carry from God, how will anyone make a withdrawal from you? She responded with the question that almost everyone asks at this point:

"Well, what does He say about me?"

"God says you are going to be a really good mum," I replied.

She began to weep. Through her tears she blurted out to me that she had just found out she was pregnant and had told no one, not even her boyfriend, and that she had an abortion booked for Thursday.

"This morning I prayed for the first time ever," she sobbed, "I said to God, 'God, if You're even real, would You please tell me what to do about my pregnancy?'"

As she wiped away her tears, a resolve began to grow on her face. With determination she said, "If God says that I'm going to be a really good mum, then I'm going to ask for time away from my till right now so that I can phone up and cancel my abortion."

And that is exactly what she did!

HARD-WIRED WITH HUNGER FOR JESUS

I believe that every dentist, hairdresser, shop assistant, pizza delivery person, nail technician, waiter, school mum that I rub shoulders with in the school playground, my children's teachers, the person on the plane that I'm sitting next to—everyone—is crying out to have a power encounter with Jesus, even though they don't yet realize it!

> *Everyone you meet is crying out*
> *to have a power encounter with Jesus!*

Hard-wired into every one of us is a deep hunger for Jesus. The great English preacher C. H. Spurgeon called Jesus the *"desire of nations."* He put a yearning for Himself in us all. We turn up, power filled, with spiritual gifts, and become spiritual midwives as people are birthed into a relationship with Jesus.

Trust me, very few people *ever* refuse a prophetic word or turn down the opportunity to have a dream interpreted, to be healed, or to be delivered when it is offered to them!

Spiritual gifts, given from the place of *all* power by the King of *all* authority, *must* find a way out in everyday life to meet all the people we interact with.

> *Spiritual gifts must find a way*
> *out in everyday life to meet all*
> *the people we interact with.*

PROPHESYING AT THE MAKEUP COUNTER

A particular favorite of mine is to prophesy over the teams that man the makeup counters of department stores in shopping malls. These ladies (and occasionally men) are always looking for conversations and interaction, and I love my makeup. It's a perfect combination!

One day a makeup assistant was helping me apply a new foundation and was busy matching my skin color when she asked me that universal conversation starter, "What do you do for a living?"

Asking Jesus for what response is needed for this moment, I replied, "I'm a dream interpreter. You have a repetitive dream about bees, don't you? Tell me about it."

She shared her dream about bees with me, and I listened to the Holy Spirit so that I could know what God meant by it.

I made a start to explain her dream to her, but as soon as she found out that it was a message from God, she began to weep so much that we had to swap places; she slumped into the makeup seat, her body heaving with tears, and I opened all the drawers of her counter in order to find some tissues!

"Does God really think about me? Does God really talk to me? I didn't think He knew or cared. How did I not know it was Him until now? Wow, oh wow! He speaks to me...." Her words are tumbling out of her, and I hadn't even begun to interpret her dream yet!

The dream happened to be about the lady's son, who had left home. Through the dream, God had been showing this precious mother that He had been looking after them both—but all this seemed entirely secondary to her in this moment. She was simply and completely undone to find out that God bothers about her enough to want to communicate with her.

That day she ran with ease into the arms of the Savior who purchased her life on the cross, even as my foundation and mascara were bought and paid for.

> ### *She was simply and completely undone to find out that God bothers about her enough to want to communicate with her.*

More Makeup Adventures

Another day, another makeup counter, and the conversation began in the same way.

"What do you do for a living?"

This time, "I'm a prophet and I hear from God."

"Oh! That's a bit different! Does He have anything to say to me?"

On this occasion, like many, it's not the length of the prophetic word spoken or even how "deep" it sounds to *my* ears, but simply that I know that I have been entrusted with power from Jesus, even in a sentence: "You have been obsessed with grief and can't shake it, but Jesus wants to heal it."

That's all I had to say, but the sentence cut deeply into her and she cried out, "My sister and friend have both just died of cancer. I can't shift the overwhelming, morbid focus on death. I used to go to church, and I believe in Jesus. He really knows me, and I had forgotten! If Jesus can heal my heart, I am going to go back to Him and back to church this Sunday!"

She grabbed me and hugged me, thrilled to be known and to be in connection with her Savior. I paid for my makeup and marveled at how Jesus trusts us with the ability to bring transformational, life-changing words in a one-minute chat.

DECREE TIME!

It's time to decree out loud over yourself so that you can hear it:

What God has put in me will change lives.

I have been entrusted with weaponized gifts from the most powerful place in all of Heaven and earth.

CHAPTER 3

Powerful Prophetic Warriors Arise!

Courage, above all things, is the first quality of a warrior.

—Carl von Clausewitz, Military Strategist, ***On War***

THE WARRIOR SPIRIT

In our great need to have more electricity in our nations, *hydraulic fracturing*, or "fracking" has been developed as a technique designed to recover gas and oil from rock. It is a relatively new and controversial way to deal with our impending global energy crisis.

The process is defined as liquid under high pressure pushed into the ground (subterranean) with such a force that it pulverizes the rock to release its resources or treasures within—oil, gas, and so on. It forces open what has been previously shut and locked away.

Just as fracking releases forgotten and needed treasures, sometimes we require a high-pressure rush of the prophetic in our lives to unmask and bring to light what's inside of us.

Just as fracking releases forgotten and needed treasures, sometimes we require a high-pressure rush of the prophetic in our lives to unmask and bring to light what's inside of us.

Each one of us has places in our lives that we don't know how to fix ourselves—the memories that hurt and became like internal coffins where our dreams and callings were laid to rest. We have hard places in our lives that require God and His prophetic people to do some "fracking" in us, to release, expose, and bring forth our hidden wealth.

We have forgotten (or perhaps we've never seen) what we were created to *do* and to *be*. The prophetic provokes our memories and shatters the walls that hinder us. It legislates on our behalf when the world spoke against us and our own history shut us down.

THE MISSIONARY WHO'D FORGOTTEN HER VISION

Some years ago we had a young missionary come to visit our center in Glasgow, Scotland, for a "prophetic checkup" appointment (I'll explain more about these check-ups later). She had recently been forced to come off the mission field due to deteriorating eyesight and was feeling like a failure. It's fair to say that she had become overwhelmed by her negative feelings and was in a total quandary as to what was next for her life.

The word of the Lord came from our team during that appointment, speaking about children's books that were within her. She had forgotten this call on her life. On her way home, as she peered out the darkened window of a train carriage, a Heaven-sent, open vision played out in front of her. It was God showing her the character who would become the central hero of her books. In just one evening, prophets had cracked open her call, and God gave her the revelatory spark that she needed to begin her writing adventure!

> *In just one evening prophets had cracked open her call, and God gave her the revelatory spark that she needed.*

Whilst with us the young missionary wept uncontrollably. As we've already seen from all the testimonies I've shared so far, this is such a common response to prophecy. Why? I believe it is because people have forgotten who they are and then the remembrance that prophecy brings often triggers a flow of emotions, like the breaking open of a dam that has been holding back a whole reservoir of feelings.

FIRE AND HAMMER WORDS

God describes His words as like "fire" and "a hammer"—like burning wood and pulverizing rock. These are all-consuming, blazing words, forging and pummeling until what stands against them is determinedly dispersed or utterly destroyed.

> *"Is not my word like fire," declares the Lord, "and like a hammer that breaks a rock in pieces?"* (Jeremiah 23:29)

God wants to release you to a new level! He wants the oil, blessing, and treasures stored in you to gush out. And often your advance to this new level only comes when a prophetic "fracker" brings a *fire and hammer word* that kindly, yet forcefully, breaks you out and pushes you upward.

Do you have hard issues in you that you never seem to find a breakthrough for? You need a fire and hammer word to break in!

> *Do you have hard issues in you that you never seem to find a breakthrough for? You need a fire and hammer word to break in!*

Prophetic words swoop down like fire and hammer to attack what the enemy has built against people. These words penetrate to every place of darkness within us, right down to our intractable, stubborn pain. These words go to war and speak into the places where devils have been grasping and resisting us, and they break us out and break us free.

Realize that there is more in you and in those you will minster to than has currently been revealed. When God releases anointed, Holy Spirit-revealed words through His people, He turns things around and brings divine transformation.

> *When God releases anointed, Holy Spirit-revealed words through His people, He turns things around and brings divine transformation.*

We are called to be "prophetic frackers"! We are called to be imitators of Jesus; we are supposed to have our mouths filled with the substance of Heaven. We are called to know what it is to speak into people's lives with love and a warrior edge that burns away their pain and *fights them into freedom*!

Do you understand the awesome fullness of what this means? This means that the very earth must respond *now* by tangibly, measurably changing when you prophesy! Your prophetic words do *not* linger in the breeze, floating about in the air before falling to the ground lost, like a solitary snowflake in the thaw.

Let me explain this with a real-life example.

THE FIFTY-YEAR-OLD ON A GROWTH SPURT!

Whilst preaching in my home city of Glasgow, I was looking in the spirit realm and was distracted by a man in the balcony who had started to reverberate with a golden glow. Realizing that this was caused by the "hovering" of the Holy Spirit, I stopped whatever I had been saying and began to prophesy over him. Words about this man's life and ministry and how his spiritual life would grow in stature came tumbling out, and then I heard the Spirit of the Lord say, "Tell him to measure his height. As a sign of what I will do he will start to grow taller and his shoe size will increase. He is to measure himself tonight when he gets home, and for the next three months he will grow."

Now, this man was fifty years old, long past the growth spurts of his teenage years, but within three months he was two and half inches taller and had to buy new shoes because he had gone up a size!

Prophecy brought about a measurable change and even broke him out of the confines of his physical body.

God gives us power when we prophesy. He expects us to use it to demonstrate His limitless Kingdom, to break open and bring into freedom people, cities, and nations.

> *God gives us power when we prophesy. He expects us to use it to demonstrate His limitless Kingdom.*

When we prophesy, we break off of people every place that they have that has been devastated and destroyed by the enemy.

There is a warrior, forceful violence that needs to rise up in us to come against the rocks in us and in others.

The prophetic is not just about saying words that massage someone's ego, that make them feel pumped up for a moment. Prophecy is not about flattery. It is not about the recipient thinking, "It's my turn for a word—bless me, bless me. Make me feel good; make me feel significant."

Sure, prophecy certainly does bless, and it will build you up, but prophecy is also an instrument of war. Prophets are fundamentally warriors, who know how to set captives free with words that liberate and fight on the recipient's behalf.

> *Prophets are fundamentally warriors, who know how to set captives free with words that liberate and fight on the recipient's behalf.*

John the Baptist knew all about this. The Bible says that he was the greatest prophet who ever lived. The main thrust of his prophetic words was, "Repent, the Kingdom of God is at hand." But he also spoke about being spiritually violent.

> *And from the days of John the Baptist until now the kingdom of heaven suffers violence, and the violent take it by force* (Matthew 11:12 NKJV).

So immense was John's prophecy and so great the change it brought, the Kingdom of Heaven suffered violence! In other words, the Kingdom of God was grabbed hold of by John and was arrested, laid hold of, pulled down, and advanced in the earth realm.

There is prophecy in you that will literally grab hold of Heaven, and the Kingdom of God suffers violence. This is not a negative thing. In fact, it is a positive, forceful interruption to the negative way that things have been going.

And many situations need *you* to speak and interrupt the way things are going! You will speak and Heaven will back you up. This is only available to those who are prepared to raid the Kingdom of God with a violent spirit.

This is only available to those who are prepared to raid the Kingdom of God with a violent spirit.

Now, I get that this is hard to read, but that's because we are so used to thinking about the Bible in a lopsided way.

For example, if you were asked to pray to be innocent like a dove, you would jump at the chance to have those words in your mouth, wouldn't you? There would be an easy flow of language that asks God for a refining that makes us innocent.

However, this is only part of the story! In Matthew 10:16 we are told to be *"as shrewd as snakes and as innocent as doves."*

Do we ever pray to be as shrewd as a snake? Do we easily contend to be as astute and as artful as a shrewd snake? Yet this is biblical language!

Likewise, when Scripture asks for violence, we have no inner hook of understanding to hang this truth on. We know *"gentle Jesus, meek and mild,"* but do we reflect Jesus the mighty man of war?

To be clear, of course this is not a biblical excuse to be rude, domineering, or nasty, but it *is* a godly instruction to be in eager pursuit of His Kingdom, a positive assertiveness, guided by God to act forcefully—not against men but against the powers of darkness—and on behalf of the people.

It's a biblical request to awaken the warrior spirit in us all. It's a call to employ the utmost eagerness and effort in an energetic and forceful seizing of the ways of God! We must think in a combatant way when we use prophecy.

God is saying: "Where is the advance raiding party who will come, like John the Baptist, and take revelation from Heaven, speak it and see Heaven back it up with power?"

"Where is the advance raiding party who will come and take revelation from Heaven, speak it and see Heaven back it up with power?"

In all of the dark situations that you face, in every place a break-through is necessary, when all about you says that the issue that you are facing is an impenetrable one and that there will never be a solution, that is when you need prophecy. God is looking for "pro-phetic frackers" who will arise and speak a breaking-off of the rocks of restriction and constraint, who will quarry a way through and, by way of an explosive raid, will establish the advance footholds that you need to get you out.

Do you need to change your prophecy paradigm?

Prophecy is not massage therapy.

- It's not a spa day.
- Nor is it a Band-Aid sticking plaster!

Rather, prophecy is the combatant words from an awakened warrior who knows how to love so sufficiently that they will put themselves out and fight with enough determination to set you free and shift you into your future.

Remember that Moses struck the rock and brought forth water out of the midst of a dry and barren place. And Joshua confronted the immovable, impenetrable walls of the enemy in Jericho. Each of these circumstances should encourage us with the evidence that, even in seemingly dead, dry, and barren situations, there is always hope.

For Joshua, God had a strategy to release a forceful, powerful anointing against what seemed impossible. This solution came in the form of a sound out of the Israelites' mouths that broke down a fortified wall! Incredibly, miraculously the people's shout fractured the walls. What does this tell us? That we don't just release a noise; we release an anointing that sits on our words and breaks down the structures and strategies of hell.

What is in you is supposed to deal with individuals, families, communities, and nations! Every time we prophesy something should change.

Every time we prophesy something should change!

When someone stands in front of us for a prophetic word, we should be asking about them:

- How free can I get you today?
- How far can I transition you into the purposes of God?
- Can I set a new horizon line in your life for you to aim at?

So ask yourself:

- Do I want to prophesy with an awakened warrior spirit?
- Do I want to rescue people and nations for the purposes of God?

Do you want to prophesy with an awakened warrior spirit?

ACTIVATION

It's time to repent for downsizing your gifts and what God has given you. It's time to partner with a new understanding of the prophetic.

Pray:

> Jesus, I am sorry for each and every time that, knowingly and unknowingly, I downsized my spiritual gifts. I am sorry for diminishing them and seeing them as an optional extra. Jesus have mercy on me. Jesus, I receive Your forgiveness.

Now place you hand on your stomach as you continue to pray:

> Jesus, from the depth of my being would You awaken my warrior spirit. Would You release me back to the cutting-edge and establish a pioneering, adventuring spirit again in me?
>
> I want to surrender all tameness and spiritual dilution; I'm fed up with the same old, same old, repetitive spiritual places I find myself in when You have made me for encounter and transformation.
>
> I want to awaken my hunger for spiritual gifts, to become voracious in my appetite for spiritual empowerments and enablements.
>
> Awaken me again to godly spiritual violence that grabs hold of Heaven and brings it to earth!
>
> In Your name, Jesus, amen!

From my home in Glasgow I am prophesying over *you* right *now*, wherever you might be. I prophesy that you will see a rise of courage and instinctive warrior capabilities become established in your life. I loose to you in Jesus's name, the mantle of a warrior champion, that you might know how to fight…and win!

Now that you've prayed these prayers and grabbed hold of the prophetic decrees I've spoken over you, it's time to deal with your inner doubts.

Who can use the gifts?

For you can all prophesy... (1 Corinthians 14:31).

This is one of the key fundamental prophetic Scriptures.

Whilst Paul is emphatic that *all* may prophesy—and most of us can at least *acknowledge* this as true—we have a harder time *believing* it.

We see the prophetic as something for those who are "special," those who know some sort of strange and mystical secret—something way too out of reach for us ordinary folk. And we have a very hard time realizing that *we* are in that special category too!

But Paul says in this verse: "Do you know what? *You* are in the special category!"

At this moment you may feel apprehensive and unsure of yourself prophetically but that's OK; you are reading this book in order to grow!

You need to establish "I can prophesy!" to be a truth that can grow inside of you, from a tiny seed into a mighty prophetic oak tree. Are you up for that?

DECREE TIME!

It's decree time again! Say this aloud:

For all can prophesy = for I can prophesy!

God has told me through His Word that
His sheep know His voice,[7] and I
can speak what He says.

ACTIVATION

One of the most important things that we can do is to take time to hear from God for ourselves, to sit before Him and practice the art of hearing Him, being attentive to how He speaks.

If prophecy is to go wrong in the context of a local church, very often it's because people have not heard God first for themselves. They then bring what is a personal word for themselves and share it as a corporate word for the whole church. We must have the discipline of hearing God for ourselves so well established that we know what God is saying to us first, before we speak over others.

So get a pen and paper and write a letter to yourself from God.

It feels very different when we take the time to write down what we hear rather than just get an inner impression. It makes the message more real to be able to read it. Ask God what He wants to say to you and record it on paper.

TOP TIP

- Don't re-read the letter as you are writing.
- Set a timer for five minutes and just let it flow.

Writing a letter from God should form the backdrop of your personal prophetic journey. Once this is achieved and mastered, you will be in a brilliant place to speak over the lives of others!

CHAPTER 4

Prophesy According to Your Faith

The smallest seed of faith is of more worth than the largest fruit of happiness.

—Henry David Thoreau

THE PROBLEM OF THE CHURCH TODAY

If you went out onto the streets of your local city and conducted a survey about the church, what would the public tell you about Christians?

I imagine they would say things like the Church is prejudiced, obstinate, intolerant, and it believes in out-of-date absurdities. Others might respond that Christians are lacking in intelligence and have no idea how irrational they sound; they stick with attempting to uphold the nuclear family with its imprisoning stereotypes but are themselves often epic failures when it comes to relationships.

You would also get those who'd rant at you that people who go to church are ruthlessly judgmental and think that everyone who disagrees with them are going to hell. Christians oppose freedom, progress, and modernity. Church leaders cover up child abuse because they care more about power than justice, they don't really value truth, they value reputation, and they are really big into controlling people.

Warming to the subject, you'd get comments such as church members get worked up about transsexuals but think it normal for bishops to wear purple dresses! The Church has provided cover stories for slavery, racism, and exploitation; it is happiest when people hate themselves and have a strong sense of debilitating shame, fear, and embarrassment.

Worst of all, they believe Christians are deeply deceived and insist on talking about an imaginary friend, a god who can be found and talked to! They get down on their knees, speaking an out-of-date language, and pay homage to some hypothetical and unreal ghost.

"Ugh! They are the worst type of people to get stuck talking to at parties!"

Would the people that we talk to tell us that we're blind and can't see what is really happening in the world? Perhaps they'd shout at our backs as we walk away, with our heads bowed low.

"Surely you all know that the Church is in rapid decline, don't you?"

"You should resign your church membership, walk out the door and go home with whatever integrity you have left before it's too late!"

Ouch! Sometimes the voices of those against us can be overwhelming, can't it?

We are the prophetic voice of God.

We are called to be His hands, feet, and voice.

We are Holy Spirit-filled people, carrying strategy for the world.

We feel dizzy and overwhelmed, trying to understand what we need to do next, because sometimes it seems like the consensus of the people is completely and utterly against us.

Sometimes it seems like the consensus of the people is completely and utterly against us!

However, there is nothing new under the sun! This is not a new phenomenon. The same things were happening in the days of Daniel, Ezra, and Zechariah:

> *Then the peoples around them set out to discourage the people of Judah and make them afraid to go on building. They bribed officials to work against them and frustrate their plans during the entire reign of Cyrus king of Persia and down to the reign of Darius king of Persia* (Ezra 4:4–5).

The Jewish people, returning from Babylonian exile, were troubled and frustrated during the rebuilding of the temple (or, to put it in new-covenant terms, they were frustrated during the building of the Kingdom of God on earth). Throughout the reign of two foreign kings, the people of God had been thought of badly, and a deliberate campaign to discredit them had been put in place. A mass movement to undermine the thought processes and effective actions of the people of God had been successful, and so their forward progress had been snarled up.

The enemy, satan, always wants to shut down the Church, its people, its progress, and its prosperity. He wants to undermine any authority you think you might have.

How should we respond to this? What is the correct biblical way to think when we find open hostility to everything that we hold dear?

We must not respond to the world today by finding a "holy huddle" and hiding away together, hoping somehow that if we bury our head in the sand that we will be rescued, that everything will turn out OK, and that God will be happy with our inaction. Nor do we want to deny the darkness, putting on rose-tinted glasses and pretending that "it's all fine really"—that's just partnering ourselves with self-delusion about how the world feels.

> *Satan always wants to shut down the Church, its people, its progress, and its prosperity. He wants to undermine any authority you think you might have.*

Instead we must want to take a stance—a position, a chosen attitude, an internally right script—and do business with the earth that God has placed in our hands!

PROPHETIC WARRIORS AND THE ISSUE OF FAITH

We prophesy according to our level of faith (see Rom. 12:6). We prophesy according to the script we have inside. **We prophesy according to what we think about God.**

*We must want to take a stance—a position,
a chosen attitude, an internally right script—
and do business with the earth that
God has placed in our hands !*

As you rise in the prophetic and prophesy things into and out of people, churches, regions, and nations, your prophetic declarations will only ever be as potent as your faith levels. Your prophetic ability will only be as good—as victorious—as your belief about who God is and who you are in Him. Your ability to turn around nations with the revelatory word of God will only be possible if you are stewarding high faith.

High levels of faith must mark and define you. It is time for faith to rise and for prophecy to rise with it! It is time to call lives, regions, and nations ravaged by the enemies' lies to order!

We need a daring faith. We need to have a faith that delights at what seems impossible, a faith that will stretch us, a faith that makes the impossible possible.

*Your prophetic declarations will only
ever be as potent as your faith levels.*

What does faith mean?

Now faith is confidence in what we hope for and assurance about what we do not see (Hebrews 11:1).

Faith is not a vain hope, it is a *sure* hope. It is not a wishful thought but is a *certainty* in who God is. Faith is an alignment, a position that we take. It is a choice, so we talk about "keeping the faith."

Therefore, we must become those who decree, "We choose to believe fully in what You say, God, and in Your wonder-working power, and we are *not* going to be moved from this position."

Faith is believing in the substance of things unseen. It is choosing to believe in the reality of what I can't see. Faith is looking into the heavenly realm and seeing what is there; it is the realization of the unseen.

Then faith realizes that what is unseen is superior (much better) to what is seen. And faith decrees or prophesies in light of this: "as it is in Heaven, let it be on earth!"

For me to live with faith is to live in a constant "aha!" moment, where it is continually dawning on me that what is in the unseen realm is *so* good, and it's right there for me to pull down to earth. And so I live constantly pulling on what I see in the other realm, the "unseen" heavenly realm.

Can we move God?

The English evangelist and miracle worker Smith Wigglesworth once said that, "If the Spirit does not move me, I move him!"[8] In other words, *he* moves God by *his* faith.

I am often asked, "Do I wait for God, or do I move Him?" More often than not, I believe that God is waiting for us to action what He has already told us to do. We waste time seeking endless confirmations because we have lost the art of instant obedience, where we action what God said when He says it the *first time*! All the while,

God is asking us why we are waiting for Him to do the things He has already told us to do!

There is a need for us to continually wake up our faith, the kind of faith that keeps us in the right place for what God has asked us to do and say.

Faith is a key component of the supernatural life that every Christian is called to lead. But if I don't have the *faith* to believe that Jesus heals, I will never expect it in anyone's life. And if I don't believe that God can change a nation, I will never speak it. If I don't believe that a life can be transformed by the Holy Spirit, I will never prophesy it.

God is waiting for us to action what He has already told us to do!

The fact is this: I will only ever prophesy according to what I have faith for. *You* will only ever prophesy according to what *you* have faith for.

Jesus shows us how absolutely brutal you need to be with a lack of faith. You need to throw it out of the room!

> *When Jesus entered the synagogue leader's house and saw the noisy crowd and people playing pipes, he said, "Go away. The girl is not dead but asleep." But they laughed at him. After the crowd had been put outside, he went in and took the girl by the hand, and she got up* (Matthew 9:23-25).

The same thing happens to Peter in the Book of Acts. Peter is faced with a whole group of sobbing widows around Tabitha and he throws them out in order that he can steward a faith-filled atmosphere (see Acts 9:39–40). This means there are some people that you cannot have around you because they are "faith Hoovers"— they vacuum faith. They suck up all the faith or seek to undermine it with their faithlessness and faithless words.

This faithlessness comes from the deceiver. But the devil is a seller of lies, and we are *not* going to buy his lies anymore! We are not going to buy into his slogans of doom and gloom and hopelessness! We are not going to hear the sound waves of hostility and believe that there is no answer. We are not going to partner with death and speak death over people and situations.

Our faith is in the God of *all life*!

We must find an ability to think about the fullness of who God is and not just think of Him along repetitive and narrow lines. His vastness must fill out hearts and minds.

After all:

Jesus saves us and keeps us, by His power, from sin and death. He has given to us the keys of the kingdom along with His robe of righteousness.

He extends His mercy, His long-suffering, His loving-kindness, His tenderness, His healing, and His compassion without ever holding back.

He restores, rescues, forgives, and redeems. He is not stingy, unkind, or out of answers. He always knows what to do and nothing takes Him by surprise.

He is our shield, our defender, our rock, and our hiding place.

He is our provider, counsellor, great shepherd, and our friend who is closer than a brother. He is the source of all blessing.

He is our victor, the captain of hosts. He is our banner and our standard, mighty in battle. He is King of kings and Lord of lords!

Jesus is crowned with glory and honor. He is our Savior, Sanctifier, and Redeemer; He is our merciful and faithful high priest.

He is the Alpha and Omega, the Beginning and the End. He was dead but now He is alive forevermore, and He is seated at the right hand of God.

He is Savior to the lost, healer to the sick. He is hearing to the deaf and sight to the blind. He is cleansing to the leper and strength to the weak. He is comfort to the oppressed, hope to the hopeless, and help to the helpless. He is a brother to the friendless and a friend to the brotherless, and He is *life* to the dead!

Jesus is infinite, eternal, glorious, and full of majesty.

One day in His courts is better than a thousand elsewhere. Wouldn't you rather be a doorkeeper in His house than dwell in the tents of the world?

Herod could not kill Him. The Pharisees could not confuse Him; satan could not outwit Him. Sickness could not overtake Him. devils could not stay near Him, and the waves could not cover Him.

The masses could not disturb Him, death could not corrupt Him, hell could not keep Him, the grave could not contain Him, and gravitation could not restrain Him!

> God has highly exalted Him and given Him a name above *every* name, and at His name *every* knee shall bow, and *every* tongue shall confess that *He is Lord of all!*[9]

If our God was who we looked at when we were wavering, if our amazing God was the object of our gaze, would our faith not also be strengthened and would, in turn, our ability to prophesy not rise significantly?

A. W. Tozer wrote, "What comes into our minds when we think about God is the most important thing about us."[10] If you think there is no solution to some of the things that you see around you, it should tell you what you *really* think and believe about God.

God is looking for a people to hear greater things than ever before, and this requires a new level of faith in us. God is on the move in the midst of us to restore our hope, faith, and levels of expectation. He is realigning us in a faith-filled position. We are to rip up the negative and depressing script that we have wrongly held onto and say, "I choose hope. I choose to be expectant. I choose to let my faith take over."

> **If you think there is no solution to some of the things that you see around you, it should tell you what you *really* think and believe about God.**

A TOP TIP TO MANAGE
YOUR OWN FAITH

*But you, dear friends, by building yourselves up in your most
holy faith and praying in the Holy Spirit, keep yourselves in
God's love* (Jude 20-21).

There is a miracle that happens to your faith when you pray in
tongues: it gets *built up*. It's little wonder then that Paul said that he
was glad that he spoke in tongues more than the rest of the church
in Corinth (1 Corinthians 14:18)! We have learned in our center in
Glasgow that hours of praying in tongues each week creates a deep
strengthening within that is hard to shake. At the first sign of any
illness, whether the common cold, migraines, and right up to more
serious conditions, tongues will build you up and create a resistance
to all the ways of the enemy, including physical sickness.

The inspirational missionary Jackie Pullinger, recounting working amongst Chinese Triad gangs in Hong Kong,[11] records the
breakthrough of many who had heroin addictions, simply by speaking in tongues.

I encourage you to start building up the time that you spend
praying in tongues. Begin with three to five minutes per day. Stretch
yourself until, over time, it becomes comfortable to go for thirty
minutes. It is such a habit now that there are a few occasions when
I have accidentally spoken in tongues rather than in English to shop
assistants!

THE GIFT OF FAITH

Let's explore the three types of faith that Scripture refers to.

1. Saving faith

For I am not ashamed of the gospel, because it is the power of God that brings salvation to everyone who believes: first to the Jew, then to the Gentile. For in the gospel the righteousness of God is revealed—a righteousness that is by faith from first to last, just as it is written: "The righteous will live by faith" (Romans 1:16–17).

Anyone who has professed faith in Jesus Christ has *saving faith*; all believing Christians have this.

2. Measure of faith

For through the grace given to me I say to everyone among you not to think more highly of himself than he ought to think; but to think so as to have sound judgment, as God has allotted to each a measure of faith (Romans 12:3 NASB).

You will probably have experienced this at some point in your life. A measure of faith is faith that grows in God through repetitive life experiences. We see, through practice and having a history with God, that He is real, good, and faithful. We see God come through for us in a circumstance and then we grow in our "measure of faith" for those sorts of situations if we face them again.

Commonly this can be seen when we begin giving prophetic ministry. We start in the shallow waters of revelation and are amazed that we even heard anything, but this small beginning helps us to believe that the next time God *will* speak. As a result, you hear Him more clearly the next time, and your measure of faith in turn increases, in step the more that you practice the prophetic. Our measure of faith goes up to believe and feel secure in hearing and communicating with God because we have practiced and have solid experiences in our armory.

> ### *Our measure of faith goes up because we have practiced and have solid experiences in our armory.*

I remember when my husband, David, and I were believing for our first ministry building. We had exactly £600 (about $750) in the organization's bank account, and of course we knew that this wasn't anywhere near enough to secure premises.

So, we gave it all away—the whole £600—as a step of faith.

Within a week of clearing out the entire ministry's bank account, we received the biggest financial gift we'd ever had—ten times the amount we'd given away (£6,000), and we were able to acquire our first rental building!

We outgrew those offices very quickly but were starting to develop a history with God. Now we had faith for doubling our rent, so we moved again into a bigger building. A few years later we grew our faith to double the rent again, and now, as I type, we have faith for our fourth ministry building and another doubling of the rent!

Our *measure of faith* is ever rising in this area.

3. Gift of faith.

Faith is listed in First Corinthians 12:9 as one of the gifts of the Spirit. In this important passage about the spiritual gifts we also see prophecy listed, which is speaking the words *of God* (not our words).

Also listed here is the gift of tongues, which is speaking the language *of Heaven* (not our language). And in the same sentence we find the gift of healing, which is using the healing power *of God* (not our power). Do you see what these gifts have in common? Likewise, the gift of faith is having the faith *of God*.

Make a careful note of what Paul is telling us: the gift of faith is not faith *in God* but the faith *of God*!

Isn't this remarkable? You can have the faith level of God through this gift of the Spirit!

This is a major shift in how we think about faith. When I strive to grow faith by *myself*, it can put the burden on *me* to come to a place of strength. It involves *my* faith, *my* ability to believe in God, *my* will, and *my* choice. Having the faith gift *of God* is very different. This kind of faith comes as a gift that God gives. He supplies this kind of faith by the Spirit. It goes beyond our faith that we can have in Him; it is God's faith given to us.

You cannot work up this kind of faith. Instead we pray, "God, give me Your faith!"

The gift of faith is not faith in God but the faith of God!

In his seminal book *Come, Holy Spirit* the Anglican Bishop David Pytches wrote, "[Faith] is a supernatural surge of confidence from the Spirit of God which arises within a person faced with a specific situation or need whereby that person receives a trans-rational certainty and assurance that God is about to act through a word or action."[12]

What area would you like the faith of God in? It's time to write a list and ask God! Will you ask for the faith of God to see cancer healed, mental health restored, or for more business impact?

You do not have because you do not ask God (James 4:2).

FAITH FOR CHILDREN

I have a faith gift for barren, infertile couples. To the best of my knowledge almost everyone has conceived who has received specific prayer from me for this. It all began with a moment when God moved on me in power at age nineteen. I was praying for an older, infertile friend. After interceding for her by myself, I was so supernaturally certain that she would get pregnant. When she phoned me. I just blurted out (in a naïve, teenage way) that it had been days since I had prayed, they must have been intimate and so she must be pregnant! She was!

> *What area would you like the faith of God in? It's time to write a list! Imagine how you will change lives as you contend for His faith to invade you!*

Thankfully, now that I have been married for twenty-one years and had three of my own children, I have adopted a more sensitive approach to these challenging areas. But back then God just unexpectedly landed in my life a faith gift to call forth children in others.

Of course, it has still always required bravery and courage to speak it out, but my faith is unshakable in this area.

Just imagine how *you* will change lives as you contend for the faith of God to invade you!

WHAT DO YOU BELIEVE?

Do you believe the Scripture that tell us that *"the latter glory of this house will be greater than the former"* (Hag. 2:9 NASB)? In other words, there is more glory to come than ever before seen on the earth.

Do you believe that Jesus is coming back for *His glorious bride– holy, blameless and without spot or wrinkle* (see Eph. 5:27)? Do you believe that one day the Church will not hurt, but will be fully healed and alive? Do you believe that "of the increase of His government and peace there will be no end" (Isa. 9:7 NKJV)? Do you believe that Jesus's Kingdom is in growth mode, no matter what any news reporter tells you?

Do you believe that the knowledge of the glory of the Lord will fill the earth as the waters cover the sea (see Hab. 2:14; Isa. 11:9)? Do you believe that all will see His glory because it will be evident and manifest? Do you believe that *"the kingdom of the world has become the kingdom of our Lord and of his Messiah"* (Rev. 11:15), that God's rule will take over and all other kings and gods will be revealed as mere pretenders to the throne of nations?

When Psalm 2:8 instructs you to ask for the nations as your inheritance (you don't come into an inheritance when you're dead; you get it whilst you are alive!), have you actually asked God for the nations, knowing that is it your Father's good pleasure to give you what you ask?

God is saying to us, "Get ready to have your minds blown!" God is going to show up; He is going to show up *in you* and *through you*. His glory will be so bright on you that people of influence will come asking you for the solutions that you carry.

> *"I will destroy the wisdom of the wise; the intelligence of the intelligent I will frustrate." Where is the wise person? Where is the teacher of the law? Where is the philosopher of this age? Has not God made foolish the wisdom of the world?* (1 Corinthians 1:19–20)

God knows *exactly* what He is doing. He has frustrated the ways of the world. Leadership looks like it is in great crisis, but God has made a space for a glorious Church to arise and fill this leadership void. In darkness it is easy for light to do its work, and so we should be saying, "Praise God! It all looks like it's falling apart, therefore, I get to shine with ease! I am here to bless the nations. I am a part of a culture that is secure forever."

Creation has been groaning for us to be revealed all along—the earth has been literally moaning for a glory solution—and the only place with that glory, the only place where God's glory is rising, is on *you*! God is looking for His spokespeople, His ambassadors, His government ministers who are appointed to act for His government in another country.

These are the days of standing out. You didn't get to be a light so that you would be hidden, but instead to be put on a lampstand. Why do think that it has been so hard for us all leading up to this point? It is because we are entering into a time when nations turn in a day!

God has invested power inside us. God has things in you that He wants to pull out of you, like He did with Jeremiah, who could speak and tear down or build up nations. God is raising up a Church that is full of miracles, justice, mercy—full of the solutions for whatever the world is facing today.

WHEN PROPHETS SPEAK A TURNAROUND

Let's return to the story from Ezra that we considered briefly at the beginning of this chapter. King Cyrus the Great of Persia and Babylon issued a decree to allow the exiles to return to Judea. A small group resettled in Jerusalem and began to rebuild the temple. However, as we read in Ezra 4, the people of God were being deliberately frustrated and harassed in their rebuilding project. Meanwhile, back in Babylon, the aged prophet Daniel is grieving (see Dan. 10), not because there is opposition and persecution to the rebuilding of the temple, but because he knows that the returned exiles are weak-minded and in despair. *Daniel is in mourning because he knows that low faith will cripple a people.* He was right to be concerned; the temple project soon stalled and then came to a grinding halt for almost twenty years.

And just like Daniel was grieving over the delay to the temple, so there has also been a grieving in our day over delay caused by low faith and weak-mindedness. Even some churches and movements have been going backward due to the crippling effects of low faith. Believers who used to be on the cutting edge have disinvited the Holy Spirit because they don't want anything messy (we should know better that the glory of God is sometimes a holy mess). Perhaps if we are honest with ourselves, haven't we also been grieving because we thought that so much would look different from how it looks right now? We thought that our lives would be somewhere that they aren't, and now we're stuck in grief.

Suddenly, God changes the message!

We find ourselves like the resettled exiles in Jerusalem, sitting amongst the beginnings of new foundations and yet stuck with our walls still unfinished! The enemies of the Jews had locked up the people, their progress, prosperity, and authority.

God turns fasting into feasting

The children of Israel had waited for seventy whole years to be freed from their captivity in Babylon, fasting and praying, year in and year out for two whole generations.

Suddenly God changes the message to Israel: "I will turn your fasting times into *'joyful and glad occasions.'*" In fact, God goes even further, promising that "people will grab hold of you and want to go with you because it will be obvious and visible to the nations *'that God is with you'*" (Zech. 8:19–23).

What caused this pivot moment, when the destiny of a nation was turned around? How did Ezra's people get unlocked from their stagnancy? What happened that broke off the people's grief and returned the forward momentum to the whole Jerusalem project? Ezra 5 bursts forth the solution into our hands: *The prophets began to prophesy!*

After almost twenty years of hopeless shutdown, two prophetic voices with high faith stepped in to save a nation, and, in that moment, everything changed.

Now Haggai the prophet and Zechariah the prophet, a descendant of Iddo, prophesied to the Jews in Judah and Jerusalem in

the name of the God of Israel, who was over them. Then Zerub-
babel son of Shealtiel and Joshua son of Jozadak set to work to
rebuild the house of God in Jerusalem. And the prophets of God
were with them, supporting them (Ezra 5:1–2).

Prophecy is a key that breaks stagnancy, breaks the stalemate, breaks through blockages, breaks down barriers, and releases forward momentum and progress back to a people. It propels forward Kingdom work and it stops the enemy.

And that's not where it stops! Turn over one chapter and we read:

So the elders of the Jews built, and they prospered through the
prophesying of Haggai the prophet and Zechariah the son of
Iddo. And they built and finished it, according to the com-
mandment of the God of Israel, and according to the command
of Cyrus, Darius, and Artaxerxes king of Persia (Ezra 6:14
NKJV).

The prophesying of Haggai and Zechariah enabled God's temple to be built and finished—successfully! (To put this in today's new covenant terms, we can say that the prophetic enables the building of the Kingdom of God in the earth realm to progress without delay and to reach a successful completion.)

The prophetic enables the building of the Kingdom of God in the earth realm to progress without delay and to reach a successful completion!

PROSPER UNDER THE PROPHESYING!

The Jews in Jerusalem built and prospered under the prophesying. *Prospered* here is the same word used in Second Chronicles 20:20: *"believe His prophets, and you shall prosper"* (NKJV).

"You will prosper" means that you will move forward, you will advance, you will breakthrough, you will become a success, you will break out, you will become prosperous, and you will become profitable.

This kind of prospering came back to a nation because of prophecy! Picture the opposite of this; imagine if we were to be silent or if we didn't have the faith that mirrors what God wants to do. Breakthrough would *not* come to our nations!

What did Zechariah prophesy to Zerubbabel, the leader of the builders?

> *This is the word of the* Lord *to Zerubbabel:* **"Not by might nor by power, but by my Spirit,"** *says the* Lord *Almighty. "What are you, mighty mountain? Before Zerubbabel you will become level ground. Then he will bring out the capstone to shouts of 'God bless it! God bless it!'"* (Zechariah 4:6–7)

It wasn't the might or power of Zerubbabel and his fellow pioneers that brought the breakthrough. It was by the Holy Spirit, released by what was prophesied.

The fabulousness of this concept of building and finishing because of the prophetic words issued must not be lost. The prophetic releases a building anointing, not just to *have* a vision but to *outwork* a vision and make it a tangible, successful, and prosperous reality.

A PROPHECY FOR YOU

When Peter says that there is coming *"the period for the restoration of all things"* (Acts 3:21 NASB), that time is now. What was broken will be restored; what was lost will be returned. We are moving into a season of great celebration as the people of God!

Just like it was for the returning Jewish exiles, the previous season of preparation can seem so slow, so arduous, and so full of resistance that we can forget what it is like to have a time of feasting and celebration. We can get into a rut until we don't even know what it is like to work with a God who celebrates. But just as He did for Zerubbabel and company, Father God will deal with your irritated, frustrated, weary, and tired heart *in a day*. It is not the promise-*making* time, it is the promise-*keeping* time. You need to know this! In one single day God can reorder your insides.

> *The prophetic releases a building anointing, not just to **have** a vision but to **outwork** a vision and make it a tangible, successful, and prosperous reality!*

Some of you started well but have grown tired, become discouraged, and have not finished successfully. Most of us have known years when the pause button was pushed in life, and what you were meant to move into and prosper in, you have not moved into. You have projects started and not completed. You have half a team and not a full team, part of the finances but not them all, part of a vision but not the full thing. You have a half-healed relationship, not a fully restored one.

I prophesy over you *an ability not just for starts and false starts but for full moving out of the starting blocks to run* a good *race. I release, even as you read this, a building and a finishing anointing to you now, in Jesus's name!*

God is putting a new word in our mouths, a fresh prophetic word in our mouths. Where previous strategies, good ideas and human effort didn't have what we need, we are going to prophesy.

God is going to give us the words to see His Kingdom built and established in people and in the nations.

We are going to prophesy to our cities.

We are going to prophesy over our governments and politicians.

We are going to prophesy over the people.

We are going to prophesy over our judges.

We are going to prophesy over businesses, so that the wealth of the unrighteous comes into the hands of the just.

> **Where previous strategies and good ideas
> and human effort didn't have what
> we need, we are going to prophesy.**

We are going to prophesy in medical centers with God's words in our mouth, and they will bring healing and life.

God says to us today: "I'm calling you back to living on the cutting edge; I'm resurrecting your radicalness and giving you back your extreme, childlike hope. I am restoring your expectation and faith."

We are to start prophesying to things that are dead and call them back to life.

We are to start calling the things that are not as though they were.

We are to start decreeing things we hear God say, and all Heaven will action what we are speaking.

WHEN GOD CHOOSES TO LIMIT HIMSELF!

One of the most outlandish verses in Scripture regarding the prophetic is:

> *Surely the Sovereign LORD does nothing without revealing his plan to his servants the prophets* (Amos 3:7).

Effectively God is saying, "I am not going to do things until I've released it to the prophets." God chooses to limit Himself to this. We want to shout back to Him, "God please don't limit Yourself to our ability to listen to You! Please don't hold back until we have heard!" But God so wants to partner with His people that He will cap His actions to what we have an ear to hear and an eye to see.

> *Start decreeing the things you hear God say, and all Heaven will action what you are speaking.*

When a nation is in turmoil, God *always* calls for the prophetic voice. Just look at Scripture:

> *From the time your ancestors left Egypt until now, day after day, again and again I sent you my servants the prophets* (Jeremiah 7:25).
>
> *Again and again I sent my servants the prophets* (Jeremiah 44:4).
>
> *I spoke to the prophets, gave them many visions, and told parables through them* (Hosea 12:10).
>
> *I also raised up prophets from among your children* (Amos 2:11).

God's modus operandi is to send prophets to nations to ensure their future. Perhaps one of the most eye-opening verses around this is Jeremiah 23:22:

> *But if they had stood in my council, they would have proclaimed my words to my people and would have turned them from their evil ways and from their evil deeds.*

If God's prophets had stood in His council, if those who were called to steward revelation had been with Him and had the faith to prophesy what was true, then a nation would have been saved! So the question is: Will you bind what needs to be bound and loose what needs to be loosed? Will you prophesy things back to life and into order? Remember, *"greater is he that is in you, than he that is in the world"* (1 John 4:4 KJV)! You get to determine who the ruling spirit is in your land, either the devil is or God is. And if you don't speak, someone else will. Who will prophesy your nation to order? There is a voice that needs to come out of you, and the enemy is petrified that you will find your voice. And that voice comes from having a robust level of faith—*the faith of God.*

JUST SAYING...

Of course, there is a caveat to all this. If all you see is gloom and doom, you've picked up the wrong script! You will prophesy death and destruction, and you will be blocked from partnering and releasing the awesome things God has for people and nations. Make sure that you're on the right script!

> *You get to determine who the ruling spirit is in your land, either the devil is or God is. And if you don't speak, someone else will. Who will prophesy your nation to order?*

ACTIVATION

If you are struggling to have faith and to believe God for the *more* that He has for you, this exercise is for you. Over the years we have discovered that having a robust list of dreams for your life opens doors of faith, hope, and expectations. Dreaming is as important as breathing. Here is an activation that raises expectation and faith levels: *Write a list of 100 dreams you have for your life.*

Now, if I were to ask you to write only four or five dreams, it would stretch nothing within you! A long list challenges you to open up your heart to expect, desire, raise faith, and come alive.

You might have some strange things on your list, that's fine. My original list included that I would love to be really good at cooking risotto, as well as the more serious things of dreams for my children, my marriage, and my work.

I did this exercise with my staff teams some years ago and then more recently. I have noticed considerable changes in their well-being as they dream with God and then are able to measure how He answers and brings fullness to the things that matter to them.

I know this will do the same for you. Dream on!

PART II

WAR

CHAPTER 5

The Believer's Authority

Authority without wisdom is like a heavy axe without an edge—
fitter to bruise than polish.

—Anne Bradstreet, Seventeenth-Century Poet

Growing up on the rural north coast of Ireland, my family were traditional, religious Irish Baptists. My dad was the local church pastor, but we had absolutely no grid for the prophetic—or even the Holy Spirit.

Nevertheless, my diligent and godly father decided to teach on every reference to satan and the Holy Spirit in the Bible, as we pushed at the doctrinal limitations of our denomination in our search for truth.

Suddenly, out of the blue, bizarre things began to happen to our family. For example, the huge chest freezer that contained half a cow and all our food for the winter broke down and everything in it was lost! Cars broke down; sickness erupted. We put it down to "backlash" from satan and his forces of darkness, after all, he was being exposed every Sunday at church in a way that we had never seen done before.

Even as a child I could already see angels and demons in the spiritual realm, but I didn't know what they were and had no language to explain this thin "veil" between the natural and spiritual. Though this terrified me for years, I still had an inner sense that our family's conclusion about satan's backlash was not right. These experiences set me on lifelong journey to understand who we really are as children of God. I started to ask questions like:

- Are we fair game for the enemy to do whatever he wants to?
- If satan was even so much as mentioned, would he really come after us?
- How strong are we believers really? What has God actually put inside of *us*?

This chapter, more than any other, expands the truth that has become the backdrop of my life. What you are about to read has radically shaped my theology and underpins how the prophecy that comes out from Glasgow Prophetic Centre sounds as it does. I believe that the truth about your authority as a believer in Christ is one of the most important things that you will ever read.

Before we continue, let's pray:

> *We cry out, Father God, write truth on our hearts. Just like You did with Jeremiah, would You put truth in our minds and mark our insides with it—the indelible, un-stealable truth about our authority. Do it for us so that we are not tossed about by every passing wave of insecurity, that we might rise up to be all that You said we should be. In Jesus's name, amen.*

POWER AND AUTHORITY

How does God rule? He has all *power* and all *authority*. Amazingly, God shares both things with us; He gives us power, which is the *capacity* to do things, and He gives us authority, which is the *right* to do things.

Apart from God we are the only beings in the *cosmos* with authority. Angels have power (capacity) but no authority (right) because they are not created in the image of God. They wait for God to task them with a job. They are then given a momentary task-orientated authority; then they return to God and await their next instruction.

> **Power is the capacity to do things.**
> **Authority is the right to do things.**

The one time that an angel began to initiate things, taking authority and right that wasn't his to have, that angel fell and became satan. Angels don't have authority (unless sent). *They only have power.*

Of course, God doesn't use demons. So where might a demon get its authority from? Demons get any authority they have from *us*. We give it away! We are the only beings in the universe with authority to discard, surrender, and to hand over.

I want you to be really clear on this: God doesn't send demons to do anything. Yes, we see from Scripture that they sometimes show up at the throne of God and God acknowledges that they exist (He asks them what they have been up to and they reply that they are looking on the earth for people who will cooperate with them *and give them authority*).

Only God and humans have power *and* authority.

Now that we've established this truth, let me ask a new question: What level of authority do you have?

> *Then Jesus came to them and said, "All authority in heaven and on earth has been given to me. Therefore go..."* (Matthew 28:18–19).

Only God and humans have power and authority.

The *"all authority"* that was given to Jesus has been given to us! And if we have all authority then it means that someone else (i.e., satan) has none!

YOU ARE MORE THAN A CONQUEROR!

We need a new mindset to deal with the vastness of this truth. The Apostle Paul builds upon this revelation by telling us we are *"more than conquerors"* (Rom. 8:37). What does this odd phrase mean? Surely we are simply conquerors and overcomers. (The reality for most of us is that we would like to feel that we lived in more successive victories than we currently do!) Let's explore the phrase using tennis as an example. Tennis has been my favorite sport for as long as I can remember and watching it has been a big part of my life. The Scottish player Andy Murray is a personal hero of mine, and he's a *conqueror* because he has won Wimbledon twice, the US Open, and two Olympic gold medals! Along the way he has defeated some of the greatest players of all time: Novak Djokovic, Rafael Nadal, and Roger Federer.

Murray gets paid the winner's/conqueror's check—it's usually a big one! The check gets cashed at the bank, and Murray's wife, Kim, probably goes to Selfridges or Harrods and buys Prada, Gucci, and all the top designer brands.

Sir Andrew Murray is a hero and a conqueror, but Kim is *more than a conqueror*! She lives out the blessing of the victorious place.

And in the same way, you don't have to fight like Jesus did. You get the easy part of choosing how to apply the winnings! *You* are more than a conqueror!

The foe is defeated, and God asks you, "What do you want to do with the victory?" The truth is that you get to declare Jesus's victory by driving out demons with a word, because at His name every knee bows. There is power in the name of Jesus, and His name makes demons tremble.

The demons are so scared of Jesus that when He goes to the land of the Gerasenes, they beg Him not to cast them out or to torment them because Jesus is a demon tormentor! (See Mark 5:1–20). His name is a torment to all powers of darkness, and demons tremble and flee before Him.

You are more than a conqueror!

We stand today in the limitless power of the resurrection. There is no cap on your life. There is no limiting factor, unless you believe that there is.

You are more than a conqueror. A greatness was bestowed on you by the resurrection of Jesus.

RENEW YOUR MIND

The call on your life is to shift spiritual atmospheres and bring the Kingdom of God into the earth. Your life is supposed to effect change and deliver Holy Spirit impact.

I know that some of you are fed up hearing about this kind of concept when nothing really changes. A new mindset must therefore come upon us and we must break out of small thinking and repetitive thinking that has kept us captive in a glasshouse, where we see where we want to go but never seem to get there.

> *Do not conform to the pattern of this world, but be transformed by the renewing of your mind. Then you will be able to test and approve what God's will is–his good, pleasing and perfect will* (Romans 12:2).

Our minds are made to be renewed and ultimately our role on planet Earth is to be a nonconformist.

TRANSFORM YOUR MIND

It is not humanly, biologically possible to transform your mind. We can *reform* ourselves by changing our behavior; we can *inform* ourselves with education; but only by supernatural means can we be *transformed*. And it is not a renewing of our *thoughts*; it is a renewing of our *minds*. God does not say in this verse, "Get a whole new thought." He says, "Get a whole new mind." That is massive!

This word *transform*, which is interpreted from the Greek word *metamorphoó*, is only used four times in the Bible. It is used in Romans 12:2, as we've just seen.

We see it in Second Corinthians when Paul writes that we are being transformed from one degree of glory to another:

> *And we all, who with unveiled faces contemplate the Lord's glory, are being transformed into His image with ever-increasing glory, which comes from the Lord, who is the Spirit* (2 Corinthians 3:18).

And it appears in two Gospel accounts of Jesus's transfiguration:

> *There he was transfigured before them. His face shone like the sun, and his clothes became as white as the light* (Matthew 17:2).
>
> *After six days Jesus took Peter, James and John with him and led them up a high mountain, where they were all alone. There he was transfigured before them. His clothes became dazzling white, whiter than anyone in the world could bleach them* (Mark 9:2–3).

The word *transfigured* in these verses is the same word that we've already read translated as *"transformed"* in the other two passages. Therefore, what happened to Jesus at His transfiguration can happen to *your mind*, and it does happen when you shift up levels of glory! Your mindset is supposed to change miraculously and become resplendent with a divine brightness; your whole mind should be elevated to a new status of thinking. When Paul writes of your whole mind being *transformed*, he is undoubtedly unpacking a truth that is not something we strive for but is instead a miraculous exchange in our heads. When we lay hands on our heads, we need to expect a shining, glory-fueled, miraculous shift. We require some serious mind changes to work with the power and nature of God, as co-laborers who have been given power and authority.

*What happened to Jesus at His transfiguration can happen to **your mind**.*

TOP TIP

Lay hands on your head daily and ask God to miraculously transform your mind so that you might grasp the full nature of who you are. This will deal with all your dead-end thinking, but more than that, it will release fresh creative strategies to you and give you the ability to move in the things God that has called you to with greater ease.

THE KINGDOM OF GOD IS SUPERIOR

We are not to put new thoughts into an old mind. We are to be so transformed that we create a Kingdom of God culture that the world can become. Scripture is very clear that the kingdom of this world, one day, will become the Kingdom of our Lord and of His Christ (see Rev. 11:15). This will be where the culture, values, and ways of the Kingdom of God will be superimposed over all other cultures.

The Kingdom of God is not an equal and opposite opposing force to the kingdom of darkness. We are not desperately trying to keep satan down; there is no equal between us and the devil!

God's Kingdom will and does envelop the kingdoms of the world. God's snake ate Pharaoh's snake in the days of Moses (see Exod. 7:10–12), because God's Kingdom is so superior.

> *The Kingdom of God is not an equal and opposite opposing force to the kingdom of darkness. There is no equal between us and the devil!*

Our fear of the enemy must be dealt with. Our being impressed with satan must be immediately halted! We are to live in response to who God says we are, rather than living dazzled by darkness. *I don't fight darkness and get slimed!* I don't eat broccoli and turn green. I don't eat cauliflower and turn white. I don't eat chicken and start to cluck! I don't fight darkness and become overwhelmed by it. It is under my feet; it is defeated.

Demonic backlash

Let's now address that concept of receiving demonic "backlash" that seems to come because we enter a battle with satan or expose him and his schemes.

At the top of the chapter, I explained that my family always felt that we were hit by counterattack whenever my dad would preach on satan or the Holy Spirit. We developed the belief that it was something like a trial that needed to happen to us in order for him to be able to teach on these subjects.

Our fear of the enemy must be dealt with. Our being impressed with satan must be immediately halted!

Years later my husband and I would lead ministry teams into New Age or psychic fairs. We would set up stalls that offered prophetic words right alongside all the witches, warlocks, mediums, and psychics offering their hundreds of varieties of readings, spells, and tarot cards. The witchcraft community would tell us things like they didn't like our aura and that we were interfering with their energy pathways (we would inform them that it was actually the Holy Spirit and give them a "well done," for spotting Him!). The stallholders would walk by us, throwing curses and generally trying to intimidate us, and yet we were always the busiest stall, with many of our guests encountering Jesus with ease.

We were once visited by an injured psychic healer who had tried every reiki, incantation, and spell-working mystic in the room, all to no avail. He tentatively approached our stall to ask us to pray for healing for his ankle. Before he even sat down in our chair, he was leaping around and crying out, "What are you doing to me!? What is happening?" as he felt the Holy Spirit put such healing heat on his legs. He was completely blown away that the power of God could just land on him like that without us having to call it up! He very quickly wanted to know Jesus.

Another time, a witch came to us for prayer and said, with desperation, that her entire coven had all fallen out with each other and she didn't know what to do. She so liked "how we looked in the spirit realm, all bright and white" that she wanted us to pray a blessing on her feuding gathering of witches as she believed that our "good energy" would help get them back in full working order!

What do you say to that? Leaning deeply into Jesus, my husband David started to prophesy about the damp problems in this precious lady's house, caused by a broken gas central heating system. He told her how God was concerned about her health and that the mold spores in the air were going to give her problems if not addressed.

She turned pale, "Does your God know about the details of my life? How is it possible that He would care about the details of what matters to me?" She was stunned that Jesus cared enough about her personal details and had such an overwhelming encounter with Him that day, that the initial request to bless her coven fell to the wayside and was forgotten!

At these New Age fairs, we saw brain tumors disappear, backs healed, and mental health issues immediately lift off as deliverance was applied.

Despite all these victories, we would go home exhausted, only to find that the dishwasher had leaked and flooded the downstairs, or that our children would be feeling sick, wouldn't sleep, and would keep us up all night. One time our shower developed such a leak that the floorboards underneath it gave way and the entire shower unit fell through the ceiling and into our kitchen beneath!

We would accept all these mishaps, upsets, and home disasters as the meddling of satan, our payback for rescuing lives from his dark realm.

Then, finally one day, it dawned on me that if I had all power and authority given by Jesus, I didn't need to put up with this anymore. The Holy Spirit helped me to realize that I was creating the problem by believing in backlash. All along, we had been the source of our own counterattack! As soon as we realized this, renewed our minds, and stopped empowering the devil, all demonic backlash ceased.

> *We would accept all these mishaps, upsets and home disasters as the meddling of satan, our payback for rescuing lives from his dark realm.*

Nowadays, I often find when I'm in traveling mode and ministering away from home that people will ask me, "Were you bothered by the demons of this region during the night?" My reply will always be, "No!"

I didn't give away my authority; I didn't surrender what God had given me and thus let the demons or principalities have space to become a problem to me. Sure, a demon might come to my room as a harassing spirit to be a pest, but when this happens, I simply tell it that it isn't allowed. And therefore, a harassing spirit becomes an *impotent* spirit by my exercising my authority and power. And I send it away!

Will we have to wrestle with the demonic on occasions? Yes, but all demons will flee as we resist them. They *must*. They bow at the name to Jesus *every time*.

*I was creating the problem by
believing in backlash.*

The only occasion that you can legitimately get mangled by the
enemy is when you take on something in spiritual warfare that you
do not have the God-given and clear mandate to deal with. You
have all power and all authority *always*, but you might not have
God's permission to deal with darkness in certain situations.

Remain obedient to Him and remember that it is *never* the case
that you lack power and authority. It is *never* that you are not strong
enough. It is *never* that the enemy is bigger than you; and it is *never*
that the enemy is more resourced than you!

God is so powerful that by the finger of God I can cast out demons
(see Luke 11:20).

*It is **never** the case that you lack power and
authority. It is **never** that you are not strong
enough. It is **never** that the enemy is bigger
than you; and it is **never** that the enemy
is more resourced than you!*

There is more power in your little finger than in all of hell put
together! The Bible says that the first apostles turned the world
upside down: *"These who have turned the world upside down have come
here too"* (Acts 17:6 NKJV). We also are to flip the world on its head
and so much disturb the patterns of hell that the enemy has no idea
how to get back on track. Our minds need to truly understand the

power that we carry or else we will back off from any and all confrontations with darkness. Backing off should never be an option for any Christian—after all, hell will not back down in its plans against us.

WE ARE THE IMAGE OF GOD

In the beginning, we read that God made things *"according to their kind"* (or *"after their kind"* in some translations):

> *So God created the great creatures of the sea and every living thing with which the water teems and that moves about in it, according to their kinds, and every winged bird according to its kind. And God saw that it was good. God blessed them and said, "Be fruitful and increase in number and fill the water in the seas, and let the birds increase on the earth." And there was evening, and there was morning–the fifth day.*
>
> *And God said, "Let the land produce living creatures according to their kinds: the livestock, the creatures that move along the ground, and the wild animals, each according to its kind." And it was so. God made the wild animals according to their kinds, the livestock according to their kinds, and all the creatures that move along the ground according to their kinds. And God saw that it was good (Genesis 1:21–25).*

God made trees *according to their kind*. Tree kind! He made the insects *according to their kind*. Insect kind! God made kangaroos *according to their kind*. What kind? Kangaroo kind! My dear prophet friend Tomi Arayomi explains that in creating living things according to their kind, God duplicates the DNA and gene pool of what is in Heaven here on the earth.[13] What is created on earth is an image replication of what is in Heaven.

And God says of His creations: "It is good." It's as if God is carrying out a heavenly "stock-take" of His earth creations; He goes down through His list, checking off living thing as it matches what is in Heaven. Bird on earth matches bird in Heaven? Check! Flower on earth matches flower in Heaven? Check!

Then, finally, God says, *"Let us make mankind in our image"* (Gen. 1:26)—in the *God kind* image! Just as He makes everything else after its kind, so it is also with us.

We are made in the image of God and also in His likeness (see Gen. 1:26). Later, we are told that Adam *"had a son in his own likeness, in his own image,"* (Gen. 5:3), and so we see that God is essentially reproducing Himself through His people, down through the history of mankind.

This concept is reinforced in the New Testament too. For example, when Paul says, *"We are his offspring"* (Acts 17:28) and when John writes, *"Now we are the children of God"* (1 John 3:2).

Embracing this wonderful truth gives us an insight into the mysteries of Psalm 82:

> *God presides in the great assembly; he renders judgment among the "gods":*
> *"How long will you a defend the unjust and show partiality to the wicked? Defend the weak and the fatherless; uphold the cause of the poor and the oppressed. Rescue the weak and the needy; deliver them from the hand of the wicked.*
> *"The 'gods' know nothing, they understand nothing. They walk about in darkness; all the foundations of the earth are shaken.*
> *"I said, 'You are "gods"; you are all sons of the Most High.'*

But you will die like mere mortals; you will fall like every other ruler."

Rise up, O God, judge the earth, for all the nations are your inheritance.

See how in verse 6 the word *gods* is equated with *"sons of the Most High."* When any creature bears offspring, its offspring (children) are the same kind of creature. Going back to my illustration above, the children of insects are insects. The children of kangaroos are kangaroos. The children of God are called *"gods"* in Psalm 82.

We must receive this revelation with humility and reverence, noting well that, of course, we are most certainly not "God" because there is only one God Most High. But we are His children, made in His image and bearing our Creator's likeness. We must grasp and understand the bigness of who God made us to be!

HE GIVES US DOMINION

The Book of Genesis describes our role on this planet when God declares that He is giving us *"dominion"* (Gen. 1:26 NKJV). The word *dominion* means to rule over, to reign, to dominate, to prevail against, or to trample. God lets us know right at the very point of our creation that He is going to make us rulers and that He is going to give us a domain. When we stay in this domain, we are kings. Adam was the king of his domain. And God did not just give Adam the Garden of Eden to rule; He gave him the whole earth. The soil of earth is where you rule.

The highest heavens belong to the LORD, but the earth he has given to mankind (Psalm 115:16).

Once God says let them have dominion, He is exempting Himself from the day-to-day governance of the earth. God has given meaningful responsibility of this planet to mankind, with the skill to rule. God is the King of *kings* (that's us!) and the Lord of *lords* (that's also us). We are *landlords.* In actual fact, we are not just mere landlords, we are world lords! We've got the whole world to rule. (So, don't ever be tempted to sing the song "He's Got the Whole World in His Hands" that you were taught as a child. It's totally inaccurate because God has given it to *you*—*you've* got the *whole* world in your hands. He has given authority to you!)

We must understand the bigness of who God made us to be!

As we *continue* along the creation narrative in Genesis, we reach the moment when God comes to Adam, bringing the animals to him to see what he will name them (see Genesis 2:19–20). God does not name the animals because *Adam is the king.* It's his job! He watches Adam to see if he will a name them as they are called in Heaven. I think that this was a test. Perhaps Adam said, "Lion" and God looked at him and said, "Well done, you did well." Maybe Adam said, "Sheep" and God said, "Well done! You are just like Me; you are perfect."

Then God *did* something phenomenal.

God came to Adam and told him to be fruitful, multiply, have dominion, and subdue the earth (see Gen. 1:28). Note that He says *be* fruitful, not *do* fruitful. Today God is pushing us to think differently about ruling, reigning, and having dominion. These are not things that you *do*; they are about who you *are*. You are a prince, a king of this world. It is who you are by God's original design; it's not something that you have to work up to.

Once you *become* a child of God, you are immediately given the power and authority to subdue and have dominion. You get to decide what the ruling spirits are in a region. You never have to work up to this; it's yours by birthright.

> **Once you become a child of God, you are immediately given the power and authority to subdue and have dominion.**

Therefore, put away any thoughts like, "If I… fasted more, had gone to Bible college, was a better Christian… then God might hand me something useful to do." You have already been entrusted with bearing the image of God.

GOD BLESSED THEM

As He created and commissioned mankind, "*God blessed them and said to them, 'Be fruitful and increase in number…'*" (Gen. 1:28). Nowadays we use the word *bless* lightly, almost a throwaway term, but the word in Scripture's original Hebrew is *barak*, and its definition is actually quite shocking. It means "to kneel; kneel down; salute; and bless; *to adore with bended knees.*"

God left His domain, came into Adam's new domain, and He "*baraked*" him. God got down on His knees, adored, and saluted Adam! God knew that He needed to teach, by example, all of earth's creatures what they needed to do when they saw the king of this domain and so He *baraks* Adam. He confers honor on Adam.

> *What is mankind that you are mindful of them, human beings that you care for them? You have made them a little lower than God and crowned them with glory and honor. You made them rulers over the works of your hands; you put everything under their feet* (Psalm 8:4-6).

All creation *baraks* Adam. As long as you are on the earth you will have dominion.

In the New Testament, Jesus, having all power over the devil, washed the disciples' feet, and Peter protested. "Why are you bending down? You can't do that Jesus; it's such a lowly place!" But as one of His final acts on the earth, Jesus was reshowing the devil the power and place of man in God's creation.

In Eden, *God baraks* Adam because the royal protocol is that when a king is in another's kingdom, he must lay down his crown. It's why the Bible says that when we get to Heaven, we will cast down our crowns before the Throne of the King of Kings—because we will be in His domain.

Where was satan?

As all of this was going on in Eden, lucifer (or satan, the devil) was already in the garden, ready to sidle up beside Eve. Why was lucifer there when Adam was created?

> *You [satan] were in Eden, the garden of God; every precious stone adorned you* (Ezekiel 28:13).

He was there because Eden belonged to satan before it belonged to us. He owned the place. It was his home; all the kings in the heavenly realms had seen him sent there:

> *So I threw you to the earth; I made a spectacle of you before kings. By your many sins and dishonest trade you have desecrated your sanctuaries. So I made a fire come out from you, and it consumed you, and I reduced you to ashes on the ground in the sight of all who were watching* (Ezekiel 28:17–18).

All Heaven had watched him be burned from the inside out, until all his former beauty was like ash. It had to be fire that burned and destroyed him because, as a guardian cherub, he had walked among the fiery stones of Heaven (v. 14). As a custodian of the fire, he had known the fire of God, and now it exploded from inside and ruined him.

God could not undo His word that Eden was where lucifer was to be. (God's Word doesn't return void. *This* means that your gifts and callings are irrevocable; once you get a gift from Him, God doesn't take it back!) God would not go back on what He had said to him and so, instead, He makes someone in His image to whom He did not make the same promise. Instead God decreed over us, saying, "You be fruitful, you multiply, and you make you sure that you subdue. And, above all, make sure that you get that snake under your feet!"

Every day from *that* moment onwards satan (who still wants to be like God) has a plan to say to Adam, "I want you to partner with me. You can't have all that I wanted. I want you to surrender to me the bits of you that are most in the image of God, in other words, your authority." Satan does not want you to have what *he* has always desired.

What rank do you have?

John outlines that the dragon (satan) and one third of the angels assembled to attempt a *coup* in Heaven. A *great* war broke out and archangel Michael and all his angels fought back (see Rev. 12:4, 7–9).

I wonder if at any point during the battle Michael turned around to God and asked, "Aren't You going to help us here?" But God doesn't fight satan, and instead, as we see on another occasion, He delegates it *to* Michael to dispute with, rebuke, and battle him (see Jude 9). (Bear in mind that satan is the second highest in all of Heaven and this is a tug-of-war because Michael is effectively firing his boss or, at the very least, his heavenly line manager!) As we read in Jude, Michael dared not slander satan. He is careful in how he speaks about a creature who *God* made, even when that creature was in rebellion.

> *Lucifer does not want you to have the authority that he has always desired.*

The important thing to note here is this: God doesn't fight alongside Michael because *God doesn't fight angels.*

That's why at the end of time it will be one single angel who casts satan into the Abyss, not God. Satan is so small in comparison to God that it will only require one of God's angels to put him into captivity for a thousand years! (See Revelation 20:1–4.)

It would have broken protocol if God had stepped in to fight the rebellious angels. It would have made the angels falsely believe that they were somehow equals with God.

There is a protocol in Heaven where everybody has a spiritual rank. Colossians lists the four levels of authority in God's Kingdom (Col. 1:16):

- thrones
- powers
- rulers
- authorities

On the other hand, Ephesians 6 lists the four levels of authority in satan's kingdom:

- rulers
- authorities
- powers
- spiritual forces

Higher-ranking angels go to higher-ranking people and higher-ranking demons go to higher-ranking people. It's why we see Gabriel going to Mary on account of her station. She was a woman of *virtue* with an important mission, so God sends His best. Similarly, a high-level messenger was sent to Daniel because of his position. Everyone has a rank.

Satan is terrified of your rank because you always outrank even his strongest demon. In fact, you outrank satan himself because *you are made in the image of God*. Every demon knows that you are a king—it's just you who doesn't yet realize it!

Your next-level adventure will start when you get this. The number of healings that you outwork will go up when you grasp this. You are a *coheir with Christ*, seated with Him, who is at the right hand of the Father (Rom. 8:17; Eph. 2:6; Mark 16:19). God is calling you to arise to the next level of revelation and understanding.

It is time for your world to know who you are; it is time to manifest as a king who has been given dominion.

> ### *Every demon knows that you are a king—*
> ### *it's just you who doesn't yet realize it!*

It is time for the sick to stand in front of you, afflicted by their demons, pain, unforgiveness, and generational curses, and for you to know who you are.

It is time for the demonic to know your name and to take note when you arrive on the scene because you have not blinked in the face of their schemes and you know who you are.

It is time for a mind transformation, so that your thinking is brilliant and shining, full of glory.

It is time for a new level.

> ### *It is time for you to*
> ### *know who you are!*

CHAPTER 6

The Church's Authority

No matter how often you are defeated, you are born to victory.

—Ralph Waldo Emerson

THE ECCLESIA

A few years ago, many of the prophets around the world started teaching on the concept of the *ecclesia*. I believe that God is restoring the Church to the way that He initially intended it, with a greater force than ever before. As a result, we need to understand afresh what Jesus meant in Matthew 16 when He uses the word *ecclesia*—the original Greek word that our Bibles translate as church.

> *And I tell you that you are Peter, and on this rock I will build my church [ecclesia], and the gates of Hades will not overcome it. I will give you the keys of the kingdom of heaven; whatever you bind on earth will be bound in heaven, and whatever you loose on earth will be loosed in heaven* (Matthew 16:18–19).

Ecclesia was first used by the Greeks as their word for a kind of people's parliament—the legislators or governors in the land.[14]

When the Romans conquered the Greeks, they adopted this word as a military word. The ecclesia was the military's specialized task force that made things look Roman. For example, if a building didn't look Roman, they would ensure it was Romanized. The Romans also added a discipleship aspect to *ecclesia*, Romanizing through education, government, family, and culture. They understood how to disciple a nation. The Romans wanted to change the entire culture, thinking, and actions of any nation that they conquered. They wanted it to look like, think like, and function like Rome.

Jesus therefore says to us in Matthew 16 that we are the *ecclesia*—the spiritual legislators and the governing senate. It is our job to make our land look like Heaven. God is calling to His *ecclesia* at this time and asking us what we are going to do about the problems the world faces. We should not be looking at our political governments because the solution is found in the *ecclesia*, the Church. The Church is the determining factor for what happens in the nation.

When the church is strong, a nation is strong. The biggest demonic assignment out there is to talk the Church *out* of being the Church!

The Church should always be leading in the nations. It is the prime leadership force. It's the only place where God puts His legislative anointing and authority. The Church is the place that the glory of God *has* landed on for stewarding and impacting nations.

The Church is the determining factor for what happens in the nation.

Sadly, right now we are leading by our neglect.

THE CENSORSHIP OF THE ECCLESIA

In 1611, when King James VI of Scotland (James I of Great Britain) commissioned the translation of the Bible that still bears his name, he had fifteen conditions that the scholars were to abide by.

One of James's stipulations was that every time the word *ecclesia* came up it was to be treated as if it were the Greek word *kuriakos*, meaning belonging to the Lord.

Kuriakos is where we get the word Scottish word "kirk" (our national denomination is the Kirk of Scotland) and is translated as "church" in English. *Kuriakos* is a good word, and a scriptural word, but it is absolutely not the full picture of who Jesus called His people to be! King James didn't want us to be a legislative body, for historically understandable reasons. We, the Church, subconsciously began to think of ourselves as a household only and not a government. We lost our ability to think of ourselves as God truly made us.

BUILD MY CHURCH

In the Gospel of Matthew we find that Jesus has taken His disciples on a trip to the region of Caesarea Philippi (see Matt. 16:13–20). It is at the foot of snow-capped Mount Hermon, and meltwater runs down through the mountain range, exiting from the rock as a spring by the city. This rocky cliff face, towering over the city, was referred to as the "Rock of the Gods" in reference to the many shrines carved into its face to honor all manner of gods. In particular, there were shrines to Caesar Augustus, Pan (the god of pandemonium), Zeus, and Nemesis. In the center of the Rock of the Gods, where the spring came forth, is a huge cave called the Gates of Hades because it was believed that Baal would enter and leave the underworld through it.

Caesarea Philippi was reviled by the orthodox rabbis and it was taught that no good Jew would ever visit there. In first-century Israel, it would have been the equivalent of Las Vegas—Sin City— but much worse than the modern city in America. In the open-air Pan shrine, next to the cave mouth, worshippers of Pan would congregate and partake in bizarre sexual rites, with statues depicting these acts lining the cave walls. Here the gods were worshipped in unspeakably awful ways.[15]

And yet, one day Jesus took His twelve disciples, most likely all of whom were in their teens or early twenties and said, "We're going on a field trip to Caesarea Philippi!" Why would Jesus choose this place, the place with the filthiest morals within walking distance of His earthly ministry?

Might it be possible that He took His disciples to the most degenerate place in all Judea in order to say to them, "I am more powerful than any of this; all that you see here is nothing in comparison to who I am and what can be done in my name?"

When David and I visited Caesarea Philippi for the first time a few years ago, I found it very difficult to hold it together. I stood at the mouth of the very *cave of hell* with tears running down my face.

Perhaps my emotional state was partly because we have called our son Peter after this passage of Scripture. But also in that moment I had remembered that my parents had stood on that spot many years before. The memories of the sermons my father had preached when he returned home came rushing back to me, sermons when the truth that he had spoken had seat-belted me in safely, ready for a wild journey with Jesus.

Did the rocks around that cave entrance remember what Jesus had said there? Were *they* crying out for the mature sons of God to do business with this truth?

I wondered if my late mum and Jesus were watching from Heaven as I stood there. Were they urging the truth of the words my Savior had said in that place to go deeper still? Deeper still to not just mark me or my father before me, but also mark and transform my children and the generations of believers yet to come, that we might all become what Jesus intended when He said:

> *I will build my church [ecclesia], and the gates of Hades will not overcome it. I will give you the keys of the kingdom of heaven; whatever you bind on earth will be bound in heaven, and whatever you loose on earth will be loosed in heaven!* (Matthew 16:18–19)

Jesus says to us today: "Go out to the places that make Caesarea Philippi look tame in comparison–there is where I want you to build My Church; that is where you can build My Church.

Go out to the places that make Caesarea Philippi look tame in comparison—there is where I want you to build My Church; that is where you can build My Church.

When Jesus uses the word *ecclesia* here, He is undoubtedly thinking about a legislative body of people; He is certainly not talking about merely a synagogue or a building, and He is not just describing a gathering of the people. Jesus is describing a government on earth.

Jesus stands at this Rock of the Gods and He calls Peter the rock on which He *will* build His ecclesia—Church. He calls us His children, the ones who will see, established through them, the legislative change that needs to come to shape this world.

I love the fact that on the same mountain, Mount Hermon, the transfiguration also occurred, where Moses and Elijah meet Jesus in the sky (Matthew 17:1–13). The prophet of Mount Sinai and the prophet of Mount Carmel meet Jesus above Mount Hermon. Moses, who stood down Pharaoh, and Elijah, who stood down 450 prophets of Baal, now stand with King Jesus, who stood before the literal gates of hell on earth and spoke concerning His upcoming confrontation with death and hell itself. He is the one who is about to stand down the kingdom of darkness in the ultimate and final victory over sin and death!

We can have all confidence in Jesus when He tells us, in Matthew 16: "You can legislate for My Kingdom, in My name, because I am about to tear down *all* the strongholds of the enemy. And *nothing* will prevail against it!"

These are the days that you always dreamed of!

The Lord is restoring to His Body the understanding that we are more than just a family. We are also a legislative ecclesia who has the authority from Heaven to change things right here on Earth.

Jesus Christ is building us as a team of legislators, and He will down-size the strategy of the enemy right in front of our eyes. We carry a governmental anointing, a *ruling* anointing, so it's not about just surviving the flood anymore, it's about commanding the wind and the waves! When the waters rise, Jesus says, "I want you to open your mouth and prophesy to the wind and the waves; tell them to be still…and then come and lie down with Me."

These are the days that you always dreamed of! God is putting some things back on track, and I prophesy that we have not yet seen an expression of the government of God on the earth like we are about to see. The Church will be the full expression of the Kingdom of God on the earth.

This will change everything.

Satan has a migraine at the thought of all this*!*

All of the tensions and bitter uprisings in the earth are a reac-tion to what God is saying and doing regarding this. The enemy is definitely not leading in these days; he is on the back foot and nervous—and so he should be! We believe in destiny and in helping satan to fulfil his destiny—to be utterly destroyed and thrown into the lake of fire!

PRAYER

Father God, I want to live in the full revelation of who You made me to be. I am sorry for all the times that, knowingly and unknowingly, I squandered the trust, power, and authority that You have put in me.

Jesus, would You write these truths of Yours that I have read so deeply inside me that I cannot ever lose or forget them. I want to take my place beside You as a co-laborer and coheir.

Jesus, thank You for all that You have placed in me. I am in awe that You would share Your image with me. Father, show me the things and the places that You want me to impact for Your glory.

For Your Kingdom, amen!

ACTIVATION

Sometimes it can be challenging to remember that we have all had significant victories already in life. Yes, you have! Some of you overcame abuse, educational challenges, rejections, misunderstandings, and bullying. Some of you achieved a little; others of you fulfilled great dreams. You were all saved by faith in Jesus Christ— that's one victory to get you started!

Write down and keep a list of all the victories that you have experienced. This will activate in you a victorious mindset and help you to stay in the place of believing God for all that He says about you ruling and reigning today, tomorrow, and for the rest of your life.

CHAPTER 7

Fan into Flame

Two roads diverged in a wood, and I –I took the one less traveled by, And that has made all the difference.

—Robert Frost, "The Road Not Taken"

I had taken my children welly boot ("wellington boots" we call them here; you might know them as "rubber boots") shopping, and they were in their usual "delightful" and boisterous form. Boots of every possible size were strewn across the shop floor, and my boys were bouncing up and down like springs had taken the place of their legs. I was harassed and the shop assistants (yes, we had been assigned more than one!) were barely keeping it civil. The manger was duly dispatched to hurry us up and out of the place. When we got to the cash register a long line had begun to form behind us, especially as forgotten thick socks were remembered, found, and added to our purchases.

At that moment, as if things couldn't get any more awkward, I heard myself say out loud, "You look like you are carrying a lot of pain." The manager serving me looked up and gave me a quizzical look, unsure if this was the moment to tell the truth or to put her head back down and do the whole British "keep calm and carry on" thing. Thankfully, she chose the former response, and with a sudden emotional gush, she told me she had just been diagnosed with a rare and crippling form of arthritis.

Inside I wanted to cheer (I appreciate that this would have been totally inappropriate) because I knew that God was about to get glory for healing a significant illness! I reached out and took her fragile hands in mine and told her simply: "I am going to pray to Jesus, and you are going to get healed."

As I silently prayed, the line spread out to form a curious circle around me. The staff gathered, my children fell unusually quiet, and we now had quite a large audience.

"Are you a reiki healer?" one customer asked.

"No, I am a Christian and God is about to heal this lady," I replied.

As prophecy began to flow, I said to the manager: "God says that you are angry with your mum, and it has gone so deep that it has become bitterness and has moved to your bones. If you would pray out loud, copying me, to release forgiveness to your mum, God will heal you right now."

She looked shocked but, nevertheless, she repeated a simple prayer of forgiveness, following my lead, until the tears fell, and her healing began.

"What are you doing?" she exclaimed. "There is heat all over my body!"

Jesus healed her totally. Everybody looked astounded to see that in the middle of the totally ordinary, God was extraordinary.

THE EARLY MORNING NURSERY RUN

One typically stressful morning we were running late for work, school, and preschool nursery. I was pregnant, flustered, and shouting at the children to "run!" and there we were, a whirling/ waddling crowd, hurtling down the street with coats half on, bags spilling everywhere, and part-eaten toast in hand. I burst in through the nursey school door, off-loading a child into the arms of whatever teacher was nearby.

It wasn't a Christian nursery, and up to that point we had never had a conversation with any of the staff about faith issues. But that morning, without prompting, Miss Tricia, the nursery teacher in front of me, began to cry. I tried to keep it nice, but inside I was muttering, "Of all the mornings to be upset, you had to choose this one!"

She whispered to me, "I have just been diagnosed with infertility, and I will never have children."

Being in an epic rush there was no time for any formalities. I grabbed hold of her and said to her, quick-fire, "Who told you that? No doctor's word is final. Children are a gift from God; it's up to Him!"

With passion, force, and without so much as an explanation, I began to decree over her: "I loose children into your womb in Jesus's name and reverse every curse of the medics' words. I command your womb to hold healthy children and for the lining of your womb to work properly now, in Jesus's name. All death comes off your reproductive organs now."

Waving my hands in a prophetic act, I pulled death off her. Miss Tricia looked as stunned as I had ever seen anyone look (and I was also quite bemused by the rush of prophetic bravery that had come out of my mouth). I said goodbye, kissed my children, and hurried out the door, off to the next school drop-off, and now completely late for work.

She and I didn't speak of that moment for several weeks until, one day, she answered the door to me, trembling, telling me that my God had worked a miracle and that she was pregnant—against all her hopes and fears!

Not long after this, our family moved home, and I lost contact with that dear teacher until five years later, the day of our youngest child's entrance into primary school. As I released him into the classroom, I looked across the busy playground at the other mothers who were doing the same.

Through my tears I caught sight of Miss Tricia, kissing her five-year-old twin daughters goodbye, as they, hand in hand, walked into the same classroom as my son.

God is amazingly kind.

FAN INTO FLAME

Did you notice that in both the testimonies above I was stressed, harassed, and not thinking spiritually lofty or helpful thoughts? I humanly responded in each moment but was able nevertheless, in a moment, to work with the truth of Second Timothy, *"For this reason I remind you to fan into flame the gift of God, which is in you through the laying on of my hands"* (2 Tim. 1:6).

> ### It is **your** responsibility to stir up the gifts God has given you.

We are commanded to *"fan into flame"* the gifts of God that are already in us. Other Bible translations say *"stir up the gift."* This means that you wake up from dormancy by choosing that which is already in you, and you already know that *you can all prophesy*! (Reread chapter 1, if you've forgotten!) It is *your* responsibility to stir up the gifts that God has given you.

Stirring is based on your will. You do not have to wait on the Holy Spirit to push you. Neither do you need to feel like you are spiritually on form. By your will you can arouse the gift from dormancy. The operations of the gifts of God are not based upon feeling but upon the decision-making ability of each of us as individuals to believe and to act.

Oftentimes at the end of a long night of ministry, someone will come up to me and ask, "Do you have a word for me?" Even in those exhausted moments the answer can be yes, irrespective of how drained or tired I am. It has nothing to do with how I feel, whether I believe I qualify, whether I feel prayed up enough, or how I started my day.

From management meeting to ministering to Muslims

Before being a full-time ministry leader, I worked for an international pharmaceutical giant for ten years.

One day I had driven across the country to meet with one of my team members who was seriously underperforming. My management game face was on, and I was single-minded and determined to bring a sharpening realignment. My colleague and I sat down together, and I was just about to get firm with her when she totally disarmed me by asking me to interpret one of her dreams.

Before I could suggest any differently, her dream was outlined to me and tears were flowing, as my interpretation gave her insight into the very broken marriage that she was currently navigating. She begged me to sneak into her house and bless it. Nervously, she explained that she and her husband were devout Muslims who despised Christianity and that her husband would be furious if he knew what she was asking. But she was desperate.

We drove to her home, and I prayer walked around it, blessing each room and asking for the presence of Jesus to descend. I anointed every surface I could with oil and commanded it to become home for the glory of God. After I left her home, I was astounded by how quickly my emotions had had to totally change direction from earlier in the day and how easy it was to fan into flame what was needed from the Holy Spirit.

My team member's husband telephoned me the next day, and it was one of the strangest calls that I've ever received: "You don't know me, but you blessed my house. I hate Christians and was going to leave my wife, but I walked in through the door after work yesterday and immediately fell in love with my wife again. What did you do? If you have special powers from your God…my mother is dying in the hospital. The imams from the local mosque are with her to help her pass on to the afterlife. Could you go and help them?"

Well, I did go to the hospital that evening. A large family group had gathered and were in the prayer room, praying to Allah. I was escorted into the intensive care unit where the mother was being treated. Politely I cleared the room, asking for a private moment with her. She was in an unresponsive state, unable to move a muscle, and had a very short time left. In the quiet of her last moments the presence of Jesus descended in that room, and I started to sing a worship song. I sang about Jesus; slowly and gently I sang a picture of who He was, as I sat by her bedside. Drawing in close, I whispered in her ear, "I know you can't move any part of your body, but would you like to receive Jesus as your Lord and Savior before you die?" Miraculously (given her physical state), she raised a frail hand

and grasped mine, squeezing it to indicate her yes as she passed into the arms of Jesus.

Your spiritual gifts are already inside of you and when the Bible says "stir them up," it doesn't mean, beg, fast, or plead with God. Rather, it's an instruction to plug in and start operating! After all, you don't ask for what you have already; you *use* what you have already received. It's time for us children of God to call time on unhelpful prayers!

PERCEIVE VS. RECEIVE

We can often feel stuck prophetically, unable to generate prophetic words, and it is because of an Old Testament way of thinking. In the Old Testament prophecy was an *event*: The Holy Spirit did not live inside of the prophets and so prophetic people *received* a word. The word came down from Heaven, and God put words into their mouths. Words were sent, words were dispatched from on high, and the prophet issued and acted upon the words as they were received.

Don't ask for what you have already; use what you have already received.

When we wrongly sit in this model, our conversations with God have a panicked tone to them.

"God, give me something—anything!"

"God, I've hopefully prayed enough, and my antenna is up the best that I know how..."

"God, I'm waiting...please, please, please speak...in a way that I can almost, sort of hear..."

"God, are You there?"

"This feels like a lottery today, God."

"God...?"

But *we* are living in the new covenant. We already have the Holy Spirit inside us so we don't need to *receive*. Rather we *perceive* what the Holy Spirit is saying as He communes with our spirit.

"But he who unites himself with the Lord is one with Him in spirit" (1 Cor. 6:17 BSB)—you are already one spirit with Jesus. So, relax, take a deep breath, and listen; you are able to fan into flame the gift of God.

> ### We already have the Holy Spirit inside us so we don't need to **receive**. Rather we **perceive** what the Holy Spirit says to our spirit.

We are wrongly taught that, when we become Christians, *Jesus lives in our heart*, or that we *receive Jesus into our heart*. This is not biblically accurate at all, although we understand why we say it (because we are often having an emotional response to Jesus). However, the reality of conversion is that we become fused and entwined and joined with the Spirit of God! When our flesh dies and our physical heart wastes away, our spirit merged with the Holy Spirit will live forever.

We must find a place in our will where we *choose* to prophesy. We cannot afford to just wait for some sort of spiritual goose-bump time. There are times coming when the need for prophetic truth will be so urgent that there will not be time to go home to your prayer closet and work yourself up to prophesy!

At the nail bar

One Monday afternoon following a long weekend of ministry, I was lying on my couch, resting. David had gone to pick the children up from school, and I heard myself say, "God, please don't talk to me right now; I'm exhausted." Ignoring me completely, God replied, "Emma get up and go to the nail bar." Like a twenty-first century Jonah I answered back, "But God, I hate having my nails done. That is not restful for me and not where I want to go." He pushed me: "Get into the car and I will show you."

Driving through our local area, God highlighted a nail bar that I had never noticed before. Of course, they *just happened* to have a free appointment slot to take me right then.

Sitting with the lady as she polished and buffed, I asked her to tell me her story. She had grown up in a Islamic state in the Middle East, and her father had been high up in the strictest Mosque in the capital. She was well-educated but not allowed to do anything with her gifts; she had written a book but was never permitted to reveal it to anyone.

My nail assistant told me that for one evening a week she was allowed to sing in a female choir. At a rehearsal, one of the choir members bravely approached her and shared her music ear buds with her, saying, "Listen to this; you will like this song." Shockingly, it was a Christian song about Jesus. She told me in a whisper:

"Just by hearing the words of the song I immediately came under a deep understanding that Jesus was real, that He was the way and, right there, wearing headphones, and in the middle of the mosque, I gave my life to Him."

She continued telling me her remarkable story:

"Heading home, I decided to tell my husband, even though I knew that it might put my life in danger."

Upon hearing her story, her husband grabbed her and asked, passionately, "Did Jesus have women?" Curiously, he had always been concerned about what he'd read about Muhammad's many wives, girls, and concubines, and it had bothered him. Together in their apartment this precious couple had somehow concluded on their own that, no, Jesus did not have women; the husband gave his life to Jesus that evening too.

By now the nail bar was quiet and all the ladies who were waxing, threading, and filing were listening as I prompted her to continue her story.

"We told my parents, knowing that this would have dire consequences. Whilst my father was furious, my mother warned me in the days that followed that people were on their way to kill us. We had just enough time to flee, and booked the first flight to the UK. Landing in an English city, we went straight to the large downtown Cathedral because where else would a new Christian go? They gave us a Bible in our language and helped us get a place to stay."

"When was this?" I asked.

"Two months ago. I only just moved to Glasgow in the last three weeks because there was available accommodation for asylum seekers here."

Holding her hand, I told her that I was a full-time church worker. At this she cried out aloud and, through her tears told me, "I asked Jesus this morning to send me a woman who He used. I've never met a woman who Jesus used, and I knew there must be some, because I want Him to use my life."

From that moment we became friends, and in the months since I have returned regularly to get my nails done (still not my favorite thing) and most of the staff are now saved. I pray with them and advise them on spiritual matters. Few of them speak English well or have easy lives but, having fled brutal Islamic regimes, they are all glad to be in a safe place with a Scottish friend who also knows Jesus!

PRAYER

> Jesus, would You wake up my spiritual gifts that are in me because You live in me? Father, lead me on supernatural adventures where, no matter where I find myself, I can always fan into flame a word from You that will change lives. Holy Spirit, would You super-sensitize me to Your voice and Your moving in all circumstances. In Jesus's name, amen!

ACTIVATION

We have learned that the Spirit of God is one with your spirit. But what does that look like? What does God's Spirit and your spirit woven together look like inside you, in real time?

Ask the Spirit of God to show you what things look like, spiritually, inside of you, where He and you join. (Please note: this will look *good!*)

It's like giving yourself a Holy Spirit MRI! Ask to see the colors and shapes that are your everyday, normal, internal spiritual reality.

> ## *We are not being asked to call down what is already amongst us!*

After practice, this is often a helpful activation to do as you walk into a challenging situation. It will remind you of how much you and God are fused as one and how secure and strong that makes you.

WORKING MIRACLES

Not only do we fan into flame the revelation and words of God, but we also wake up the gift of healing.

There is a wrong thought often held in the Body of Christ that we are waiting for God to do something in a sovereign way and we will get to sit back and watch what happens as observers. But this is the time for partaking, when God will move *with* us and *through* us. Revival is here and revival is now in the nations. We are being asked to grow it up; we are not being asked to call down what is already amongst us!

God shouts over us, "Wake up and take the steering wheel of the ship that I have asked you to maneuver. You get to choose the direction the rudder goes in. Are you sailing backward or is there an intent within you to sail into fullness? It is time for mega-power, mega-souls-harvested, mega-miracles, mega-advance, mega-revelation. It is time for *national miracles*, and they will all come through your hands."

We are called to be a holy people (see 1 Pet. 2:9). What is the opposite of holy? The opposite of holy is not sinful or evil. The opposite of holy is being *ordinary*. Holiness is not only freedom from sin; it means sets apart from the ordinary, elevated above the norm.

The first time the word *holy* appears in the Bible is in Genesis 2:3 when God makes the seventh day—sabbath—holy. He set this day apart as special, different, and out of the normal pattern. *You* are not normal, ordinary, everyday, or average. You are the people who can perform miracles; you are set apart for the purpose of revealing all that Jesus is!

We have been used to a church that postpones everything. We don't come to church with any sort of expectation that miracles will happen.

A Jew doesn't go the synagogue and expect someone to come out of their wheelchair.

A Hindu doesn't go to the temple and expect blind eyes to open.

A Muslim doesn't go to the mosque and expect the dead to be raised.

But a Christian should expect all these things in church. Miracles are a major part of how we are different!

People should hear rumors that healing is happening in church and so turn up on our doorstep. Instead, we have a developed doctrine of excuses. We have learned to live mostly in the church with few results.

The issue is that miracles don't just happen. We must *work the miracle*. Are you familiar with Acts 19:11? *"God did extraordinary miracles through Paul."* The original text of this verse says that God did extraordinary miracles *"by the hands of Paul."*

Miracles are a major part of how we are different!

Do you work miracles? Please remove from your lips any response that says, "I'm not ready!" There is a call to renew our expectation of how much God wants to pull out of you because He has spent years investing in you. After all, you did not walk through all that you came through to *not* be a resource for His Kingdom!

ACTIVATION

Lay your hands on your head and cry out loud, "God renew my expectation of how You will use me!"

At this time in history we must learn to make a demand on God. When facing a challenging situation in your life, or the life of a friend, ask God, "What part do I play in the miracle that is needed here?" All children of God can work miracles—all can work *every* miracle! So never say, "That's not my gift!" *All* the gifts are for *all* the people!

EAGERLY DESIRE

Now eagerly desire the greater gifts (1 Corinthians 12:31).

But covet earnestly the best gifts (1 Corinthians 12:31 KJV).
Desire spiritual gifts, especially the gift of prophecy (1 Corinthians 13:1 BSB).

Desire is a strong word. One Bible version literally translates this as *"zealously lust"* after the gifts! It means that we must be in hot pursuit of the gifts and eagerly go after them until they manifest in our life.

All children of God can work miracles— all can work *every* miracle!

Surely this seems selfish, greedy, or unbalanced, lacking in discrete moderation and wildly improper to be in Scripture. Yet you must *covet* spiritual gifts! We have had too much of a false humility over this. We have told ourselves that we are not deserving of this high spiritual prize. Of course, you are not worthy in and of yourself, but Jesus *has* made you worthy, and He has commanded you to desire!

Who of us wakes up and says, "I just really want to lust after God and His gifts today?" Probably few of us; it is not in our vocabulary, but it *is* in the vocabulary of Scripture! So, if you want to kill every religious spirit within you, say out loud where you are right now, "I'm lusting after spiritual gifts!"

Our prayer should be, "Oh God let me see what You have to show me, let me hear Your voice, and let me sense the moving of Your Spirit. God, I want *all* that You have for me, and I don't want to miss a thing!"

Normally we might muse, "Well if God wants me to have it, it will come to me." Or perhaps on our super-spiritual days, we might postulate that, "If He predestined me before the foundation of the world, then it will manifest in my life." Maybe you prefer my Northern Irish granny's version, "What's for you won't go by you."

But we are told to *lay hold of, seize,* and *apprehend* the Kingdom, to covet gifts. It takes some ferocity on our part. I think some of us are too pseudo-spiritual for this; there is a mock meekness going on! Is your false humility in overdrive and causing you say, "I'm not worthy of anything"? You must be aggressive about some spiritual issues, remembering that *"the kingdom of heaven suffers violence, and the violent take it by force"* as we considered in an earlier chapter (Matt. 11:12 NKJV).

I have three children, ages 17, 13, and 11. On Christmas Day they do not wait in their beds and say, "Brethren, do we have a witness amongst us to get out of bed?" They are straight down the stairs like rockets! They don't then stand solemnly around the tree, agreeing together that "yes indeed, Mummy and Daddy are truly good indeed." No, they just dive right in and open presents that aren't even for them—as long as they are getting the biggest in the pile! The Bible doesn't say, "Only desire gifts that belong to you." It says, "Desire spiritual gifts!" There is no room for self-depreciation and not being in full pursuit of all that God has laid out for you.

JACOB AND ESAU

Jacob I have loved, but Esau I have hated (Romans 9:13 NKJV).

This is a deeply disturbing verse, to consider that God could hate someone. It brings a chill to our bones, doesn't it? What on earth did Esau do that resulted in the God of compassion and mercy *hating* him?

Jacob who, on the other hand, was loved by God, deeply coveted the birthright that belonged to his brother. He went to great lengths in an alarming and deviously designed plot with his mother to trick his father into giving the birthright to him. It doesn't seem fair, does it? The biblical birthright represented spiritual blessing and authority. Jacob was so consumed with the desire to have this that he destroyed all family relationships in the process.

How could God love someone who was so blinded by his desire for spiritual blessing and authority? This is counterintuitive to our human ideas of proper behavior and motivation.

But while it may offend us, God loves this kind of heart. God loves those who so hunger for His power, presence, and authority that they are willing to do *anything* to get it. "Jacob I have loved."

I challenge you to crave something godly and see how God rewards you with it!

Hated Esau was so preoccupied with the natural realm that he despised spiritual things. Likewise, in our human reasoning we esteem those who are conservative, balanced, and proper. But God has a different standard. He *hates* the attitude of those who do not esteem His power, His presence, or His blessing as being worthy of their attention!

When I was growing up in church, we used to sing an old hymn that I now consider a heresy. We sang, "I seek the giver not the gift."

A much more biblically accurate statement would be, "I seek the giver *and* the gift."

Desire is a scriptural key to receiving from God. Consider these verses:

> *Take delight in the LORD, and he will give you the desires of your heart* (Psalm 37:4).
>
> *Therefore I tell you, whatever you ask for in prayer, believe that you have received it, and it will be yours* (Mark 11:24).

I cannot stress this enough: God delights to give good gifts. I challenge you to crave something godly and see how God rewards you with it!

Are you willing to earnestly desire and zealously lust after the gifts of God?

PRAY

> Jesus, would You awaken a desire in me for the gifts of the Holy Spirit? I want to make Your gifts my high priority.
>
> Holy Spirit, I want to partner with You to see Your power flowing out of me! Let my mouth be filled with prophecy, my hands with healing. I want to operate with a right desire for spiritual things and not get preoccupied with the natural realm.
>
> Father God, please retrain my focus to be on what matters to You.
>
> In Jesus's name, amen!

PRACTICE THE GIFT

Now that you know that you are fanning the gift into flame, perceiving what is already in you, choosing to work the miracles, and desiring spiritual gifts, what is next? Practice.

Champions keep playing until they get it right.[16]

—Billie Jean King, tennis giant

Many years ago we had a backed-up list of clients waiting for a prophetic appointment at our center. In order to help reduce the size of the backlog, my colleague and I did seven hours of prophecy straight. We prophesied over a lot of people that day. As we spoke into people's lives, God gave me a different two-digit number for each client. It wasn't obvious why, so I began to probe Him, "What are You talking about God?" With no wisdom on it given to me in the moment, I left it alone. At the end of the night I went back to ask God what the numbers had meant, and He told me, "I was scoring your prophetic words out of 100!"

I wasn't very happy about this, but at least the numbers were getting higher with each client! I inquired of God, "Who scores 100/100?"

He said to me, "Samuel. Not a word he spoke fell to the ground. And I called John the Baptist the greatest prophet who ever lived."

Growing more curious, I asked how Jeremiah scored on his off days when his humanity was on full display. "After all Your Word tells us that we only see in part…and what about Hosea?"

God laughed.

God was showing me that the more I prophesied, the better I got at it. The more hours that day that I gave myself to listening to Him and speaking out what I heard, the more skilled I became.

There is a lifestyle that produces good quality prophecy.

When I first met my husband, he was studying for a music performance degree at the University of York. I would dash over to the music practice rooms after my politics lectures and peer through the windows to see if he was there; he invariably was. For six-plus hours a day, David practiced and practiced his trumpet—endless scales, studies, and lip-building exercises, going over and over the same bars, hour by hour. When he had strengthened himself in the scales, the basic building blocks, then and only then could he play the most amazing classical works. When we were first married, he would even practice his trumpet in bed!

There is something that happens on the inside of you when you practice what you already have. The principle of Jesus's Parable of Talents illustrates this—use what you have, and you will be given more.

> *Whoever has will be given more, and they will have an abundance. Whoever does not have, even what they have will be taken from them* (Matthew 13:12).

The promise here is remarkable. When you start to use what you have, you walk into abundance. When you don't use it, it is taken away. The more I use the gift of prophecy, the more my spirit and mind come into alignment with Heaven and the more I see and experience. There is an ongoing pattern here of practice, practice, practice, promotion, practice, practice, practice, promotion.

(After) Midnight in Malta

One summer vacation a few years ago our family was staying on the Mediterranean island of Malta. One warm and still night I was woken up in the early hours by loud shouting coming from a nearby house.

"You are killing me!…You are hurting me!" followed by screams of pain.

Leaping out of bed, I shook David awake, urgently telling him to look after the children and calling over my shoulder, "I am going to be a solution."

> *The more I use the gift of prophecy,*
> *the more my spirit and mind come*
> *into alignment with Heaven and*
> *the more I see and experience.*

Running down the street, I knocked on the big wooden door of the house that the noise was coming from. A small voice called nervously from inside:

"Who are you? Are you the police?"

"No…I'm not…"

I had a split second to know how to answer the question in a way that would see the door open safely. Normally I tell people something crazy like, "I am a prophet; I hear from God for a living." Very rarely do I ever say something as straightforward as, "I'm a Christian minister who runs a church."

Anyway, this time out of my mouth came, "I'm a church minister…"

At this the door flew open and a woman fell into my arms!

"I've been praying for a church minister to knock on my door for the last twenty years!"

Entering the woman's house, I discovered a teenage boy who had been beating up his mum and sister. Despite the noise, all seemed OK, though emotional. From down the street I could hear David praying in tongues outside our house, the sound carrying on the still Mediterranean night air, his way of lovingly but subtly letting me know that he was nearby.

The mum asked me to lead her back to Jesus, so at 3:00 a.m. she now fell into the arms of her Savior, as her children looked on. Suddenly at the sight of this, her young daughter spontaneously started coughing up a demon as she felt the presence of Jesus! I had to temporarily pause the usual salvation prayers in order to get the demon off the girl's throat so that she could breathe properly again. She too gave her life to Jesus.

The teenage boy, who had been very quiet up until this point, now appeared back on the scene, walking toward me unprovoked. With wet tears on his cheeks he now wailed, "I have anger in my heart. It's like broken glass inside me. Can Jesus get it out?"

In that moment of confession, he got beautifully saved, healed, delivered, and filled with the Holy Spirit. At this, he fell down into my arms, and I suddenly had a thought: "What on earth am I wearing?"

I was ministering in my summer nightwear—barefoot and messy-haired in the middle of the night. In all the safe prophetic protocol documents I have written for best practice ministry, never did I think to add the instruction: Never minister in pajamas!

It was only because of practicing the prophetic that, in a moment when it mattered, I could hear God clearly enough to be useful to Him. A history of prophesy with God had been built.

My practice started for me when I was working in pharmaceuticals, long before I knew that I was a prophet. I spent hours in the car, and so I would pick someone out as I drove past and would speak out loud a word of revelation, as if that stranger was sitting right beside me. I prophesied over each passerby the things that I would have said over them had we been in a prophetic appointment together. God and I played together, as I repeatedly fumbled to wrap the English language around Holy Spirit utterings. I was finding my prophetic language in private.

This kind of practice is still something I do even now, years later. If there is no one to prophecy over and I'm in the park walking the dog, then the land or the trees will get a word—or the walls and carpet of our house! Alone in the car I love to drive with the windows down, telling the clouds what they will see and decreeing what will happen on the land.

The ten thousand–hour rule

It is well documented that you need ten thousand hours of deliberate practice to reach an elite level of performance. Research shows that even the most gifted performers need a minimum of ten years (or ten thousand hours) of intense training before they win international competitions. Athletes, musicians, and chess players aim for these sorts of hours to become champions. You can guarantee that Andy Murray put in his ten thousand hours before he won the US Open!

Malcolm Gladwell, the New York social commentator and best-selling author calls ten thousand hours the "magic number of greatness."[17]

Prophetic warriors must train themselves, until the last voice they hear at night is God's, and the first thing they wake up to is the sound of the Holy Spirit whispering in their ear.

> **Practice so that when it really matters, you know what God thinks in a heartbeat.**

Practice makes perfect, but only if the practice is stretching. If your practice is unchallenging and routine, it is time to shake things up. To really get good at something, the *quality* of your practice is probably the thing you should focus on most.

To put it another way: practice should freak you out a bit. Walking up to the school gate or approaching the cash register, find the hardest person to prophesy over and ask if you can you practice on them. With checkout operators in supermarkets, I find that a good way to practice is hearing God for a single fact. I tend to go with something like: How many children do they have? If I'm wrong all that happens is that they think I'm weird. If I'm right, it opens up a conversation about hearing from God!

If the ten thousand-hour rule sounds daunting, what about a ten-minute rule? Prophesy for ten minutes a day, in the house, in the car, in the office, wherever. Practice so that when it really matters, you know what God thinks in a heartbeat. Could you commit to that?

Breaking curses in the supermarket

Recently I dashed into our small, local supermarket to quickly grab a sandwich. The man in front of me in the line to pay was dressed in long, black, intimidating robes, and I overheard him tell the woman on the tills, "I am a psychic, and I am going to tell you your future." His demonic words slimed and cursed the girls as he spoke of sicknesses, family death, and failures. By the end the women were clinging to each other, startled and scared. He left.

Immediately I grabbed their hands: "Don't worry! I am a prophet who hears from the one true God, and I break every curse that was just raised against you. In the name of Jesus, I speak life!"

And then I started prophesying the brilliance of their futures according to the Holy Spirit. Their relief was palpable. They were gushing with appreciation for rescuing them. I paid for my sandwich and left; all this was done in under fifteen minutes.

Intentionality

As you stretch your muscles to prophesy for ten minutes every day, a constant flow of conversation back and forward between you and God will naturally develop. At the outset of this process you will need to be very intentional. Intentionality looks like this:

- "God what are You wanting to do in this church service today?"
- "God what shall I decree over my children's school today that is in line with what You are saying?"
- "What are You praying for me, Jesus?"

(This question, asking Jesus what He is praying to the Father for *you*, is particularly powerful. It's a life-changing question that takes your focus off your own agenda and tunes you into Jesus's priorities).

- "God what do You think about this shopping mall?"
- "God what are You thinking about for my office today?"
- "What are You excited about today, Jesus?"

This is intentional practice. At first it is awkward, then it is normal, then instinctive, and finely it is compulsive. Once prophecy is compulsive, it becomes who you are, so that you prophesy without even realizing it. Here's an example.

Ordering ramen in a noodle bar, I heard myself say to the waitress in a stream of consciousness: "I would like extra coriander (cilantro) with that because it's my favorite flavor. I think there will be coriander in Heaven."

At this I looked at my own tummy, thinking, "Where did that last sentence come from?" I know that it's a ridiculous thing to say.

In an embarrassed reply, the waitress said, "I think there will be mushrooms in Heaven because they are my favorite!"

I'm wondering how we got to this strange conversational place, when suddenly she says, "I have been thinking lots about Heaven recently but haven't had anyone to talk to. I don't suppose you know about it?"

Boom! And there's why the Holy Spirit started that dialogue! Of course, my reply was an excited, "Yes, I happen to know all about it!" And she encountered Jesus mid-shift that day, whilst carrying dishes of noodles and gyoza.

The utter joy of all of this is that no matter where you are or how ready you feel, once you have developed a lifestyle of practice, you will find that prophecy leaks out at every moment!

Flying prophecy

Coming home exhausted on a late-night flight, I was thrilled to find that the plane was the emptiest that I had ever been on—lots of room to stretch out and relax! One of the very few other passengers boarded a little while after me, and as she walked up the aisle, I thought to myself, "Oh boy, she is loaded with addiction demons!" I'm sorry to report that I was just a little pleased and relieved when she took her seat a few rows in front of me, and I could prepare to curl up and have a bit of a nap in perfect peace.

> *The utter joy of all of this is that once you have developed a lifestyle of practice, you will find that prophecy leaks out at every moment!*

As I was about to slide down in my seat and close my eyes, she turned around and popped her head up above her seat.

"Well, it looks like it's just you and me in the back of this plane," she called cheerily across the rows between us in an Irish accent. "What do you do for a living?"

Oh boy, another Irish woman. We talk a lot. My usual reply, "I'm a prophet; I hear from God."

Well, would you know, like a shot she was out of her seat, buckled herself right in next to me, and was now completely in my personal space, asking, "What does He have to say to me?"

Trying to look happy at this question (is it OK that I'm honest with you?), I replied with a hopefully-not-too-weary sigh: "Well, God is concerned about how much you're hurting because of your recent relational breakup, and He would like to heal you."

She looked at me with a quizzical, yet intense stare and declared, "OK. I would like to give my life to Jesus now."

I blinked with amazement at this curveball she'd just thrown me. Quickly gathering my thoughts, we began the conversation about sin and repentance, all of which she was totally up for. I led her in a prayer, and as soon as she received Jesus and before I could say anything else, she asked: "I would like that language that Christians have."

The gift of tongues I explained to her, and as the Holy Spirit exploded over her, she started to shout loudly in tongues like a river in full spate! At this the cabin crew all gathered around us (after all there were not many other passengers to look after), and as they looked on open-mouthed, the lady slipped down her chair and onto the floor, wedging herself awkwardly between our row and the one in front. Stuck down there, she now entered an open vision and exclaimed, "Jesus is walking up the aisle toward me!"

Bless them; all the cabin crew turned to look, utterly bemused at the seemingly empty aisle.

Eventually the commotion died down and I got her back up onto the seat next to me.

"I have an addiction problem," she said.

"I know," I replied.

And she got delivered of the spirit of addiction.

I cannot think of a better way to spend your life than as a conduit for the voice of God.

PRAYER

Pray this only if you really mean it.

> Jesus, I want to pledge myself to a lifestyle of revelation. Would You lead me into the habit of hearing You? I want to be one who commits to the art of practicing saying what You say and that, no matter where I am, I am available for You to use, no matter how I am feeling. In Jesus's name, amen!

ACTIVATION

Find five people to practice on in the next month (make sure that they are people who like you!):

- Tell them that you are learning how to prophesy.
- Ask their permission for you to practice on them (permission is *really* important!) and time yourself giving them a word.

If you can speak for ten minutes, it will really stretch your revelatory muscle.

CHAPTER 8

Finding Your Voice—the Battle for Your Sound

You can't find your voice if you don't use it.

—Austin Kleon,
New York Times Best-Selling Author

GOD GOVERNS WITH HIS VOICE

The centurion replied, "Lord, I do not deserve to have you come under my roof. But just say the word, and my servant will be healed" (Matthew 8:8).

Above everything else, satan wants your voice silenced. The battle for this epoch of time is over your sound.

Our God rules by His voice; He rules by sound. He governs the universe by speaking to it; He uses language to shape the world. It is His voice that creates. We, His creation, reflect Him and are in His image when we speak and make a sound. It is time to understand the power of the spoken word.

God has authorized you to speak on His behalf. You are the only part of creation who is tasked to do this. No animal, no fish, and no bird was given this role.

The only reason God gave you a mouth was so that you could release power! Satan has to obey your voice; satan is your slave, and you are his master.

It is time to understand the power of the spoken word.

We have always used our voices for conversation, and now we need to use it for legislation. Your voice registers in two realms: firstly, through *conversation,* you communicate in the earth realm. Secondly, your voice *legislates* to bring down principalities in the spirit realm!

Just like God, you are a talking spirit. Your authority in the spirit realm is massive, and the spirit realm pays close attention to your voice. In fact, sometimes more so than the natural realm because when you speak by the Spirit, you speak on behalf of God. No wonder the enemy has spent so long working to silence you!

Words are given much more significance in biblical Hebrew than in the Greek/Hellenistic worldview, but today we mostly operate with that Greek mindset (or a *Greco-Roman* mindset). Whilst God governs through words, the Greek mindset expects you to govern by reading, thinking, scholarly works, and written exams. The Hebrew (Hebraic) mindset operates with decrees and words that create. To express this in another way: God fixes things with His mouth and not with His hands. This is what we are to mirror.

THE VOICE OF THE CHURCH

In this epoch of time we will see the Church get back her voice. God's opinions will be heard and spoken by His people.

This is a time when we will fight and win over our voices, a time when we find the keys that unlock the padlocks that have been sitting over our throats. An end is coming to the battle that has seen the Church on the back foot vocally. The spokesmen and women of God will arise!

If you have ever felt a reluctance to prophesy, take heart. God is shifting you out of reticence and into feeling compelled to prophesy. Yes, God is releasing an unusual anointing, where the church will be compelled to speak, compelled to decree, and compelled to declare!

This is a time when the spokesmen and women of God will arise! We are moving into the days where revelation cannot be withheld.

We are moving into the days where revelation cannot be withheld. We will speak, not when we feel ready, but when God says. We will speak at the same time as God, and it won't be dependent on whether or not we like it.

If you had lived during biblical times and had heard God say, "Walk around Jericho seven times," as He said to Joshua, would you have told the people and actioned the command? Or would you have said, "Ooh, that's very strange; I think I'll wait with this word," then let it germinate for a few weeks before deciding to interpret it symbolically?

We have been prophetic in the same way that Jonah was for a long time. Like the reluctant prophet, we have been wrestling with finding our voice and internally arguing with the call to be Heaven's spokespeople. We have fought to *like* what God says and to find our revelatory flow.

The world in this generation has never really tasted the Body of Christ, but the world needs to see that His people, His church, taste good and that there is something sweet and victorious that we have to bring to the table.

They will taste and see the goodness of God as we speak the truth. Truth will come to be seen not as an offense to the world, but as redemptive and necessary. Truth will be pleasing and urgently desired. *You* have a particular taste and sound about you that God is getting ready to present to the earth!

This is why you are being purified at the moment. You are squeezing through a narrow gate in order to be presented to the world as a voice. You might feel hard pressed on every side right now, but you will not be crushed! God is making things right for His people and making His people strong to speak.

Be sure that you do not give voice to unbelief at this time because

- principalities will be uprooted by the voice of the church;
- power structures will be torn down;
- institutions will be destroyed;
- human rulers will be overthrown;
- God's Kingdom will be built up;
- God purposes will be established; and

- people will welcome the voice of the Church and the freedom that it brings.

The Church will speak calling for the passing away of all the current unhelpful structures. Now is the time to release a new decree! It is not a time to be speechless but to have the right words, at the right time, on your lips.

> ### *You are squeezing through a narrow gate in order to be presented to the world as a voice.*

Words of power

The world is waiting for words to come from the Church that will create good things and bring restoration.

Most believers are very familiar with the promise, *"For nothing will be impossible with God"* (Luke 1:37 NASB). Nestled in the original Greek of this verse is the word *rhema*, which means "a thing spoken, a word or saying of any kind, as command." It refers to a spoken word made by a living voice. Therefore, a more literal way to translate this verse might be: *"For no word spoken by God is without power; no word spoken from God is impossible."* In fact, the most recent NIV translation now records this verse as, *"For no word from God will ever fail."*

When God speaks, we need to say what He says, knowing that His words will *never* fail. God's words in His mouth have the same weight as God's word in *our* mouths.

Words of justice

We are in a time when we will hear and read strong prophetic words that even include the justice and judgment of God, where people of revelation will outline the biblical truths of sowing and reaping or of the consequences of national actions.

In Jonah, a word of judgment produced the desired outcome of God's plan for Nineveh. The words that we release will bring about the holy provocation that nations and situations require. Justice is an intrinsic part of who God is, and it is what keeps His throne in place. God uses judgment and justice to further His plans for nations, so that they ultimately might be with Him.

We all know from our own personal experiences that we don't learn well in the times of blessings and lavish abundance. Instead we learn well in the pruning, clipping, and trimming, in the wrestling and in the pain. It's no different for our nations. If I were to ask you, "What was your key major learn of the last year or last five years?" I'm sure that on the whole you would tell me about something that you were taught because you faced a trial, a consequence, or a hardship.

> *God uses judgment and justice to further His plans for nations, so that they ultimately might be with Him.*

Of course, "God is good" but don't forget that running alongside this important truth He also has a parallel train track that keeps the Kingdom of God in balance. His mercy and goodness always run alongside His justice and holiness. We will have to say some challenging things on occasions.

"PROPHETIC PEOPLE WILL SPEAK"—A PROPHECY

There will be a fresh prophetic move of God. The prophetic is undergoing its greatest change in decades. Revelation will no longer be rare. It will be fiery, and there will be a new accuracy to it.

In the places that the church is reclaiming, for example, purity in nations, abortion laws and righteous leaders, it will be with words that are strong like a sharpened plough. And the hard ground will suddenly be broken up. Prophetic people will be instruments with teeth. They will be more frequently releasing revelation, publicly and privately, that exposes, judges, and ultimately redeems.

We will be living in a revelatory ocean, not dipping in and out, not warming ourselves up. We will be so in the presence of God as a lifestyle that we will prophesy for thirty, forty, sixty minutes straight, with the windows of Heaven open and downloads pouring over us. Those who have been nervous about the prophetic and who have never prophesied will overflow with revelation!

> *In the places that the church is reclaiming…*
> *it will be with words that are strong*
> *like a sharpened plough.*

There will be a rush of people who flow with prophetic revelation. You will lose your fear of being a bold truth-teller.

"Fear of your own voice will be broken; fear of failure will be broken, and I will take over," says the Lord.

The stifling of the prophetic will be no more, and you will prophesy like never before.

"Say yes to Me using you more prophetically," says God.

Both the prophets and those with a prophetic gift will receive the revelatory upgrade, right now.

Words of knowledge and power that bring life will come forth. Your voice will command the impossible to come to pass.

Your mouth will become a house of intense revelation. "I will live in it," says God.

Your mouth will become a house of creation. Through the words that you speak will be a new anointing coming forth to create what has not been before to create the miraculous!

The prophets will speak, and an end will come to the silence of the prophetic people in secular public places.

WORDS STRENGTHEN A NATION

In Numbers 23 we read the curious story of prophet Balaam and the Moabite King Balak, two men wrestling over what should be said to secure the victory in a nation.

The king commands the prophet to curse his enemy Israel to weaken her with words so that he might win the war over her. But the prophet point-blank refuses. Outraged at this insolence, King Balak cries, *"What have you done to me? I brought you to curse my enemies, but you have done nothing but bless them!"* (Num. 23:11).

Again, the king urges Balaam to curse, this time offering him money as a reward. There is another, second refusal from the prophet, accompanied by some stinging words:

> *God is not human, that he should lie, not a human being, that he should change His mind. Does He speak and then not act? Does He promise and not fulfill?* (Numbers 23:19)

In other words, Balaam is saying that whatever God says, happens. He is not like us. Each word of His is acted upon, each promise fulfilled. I am not going to be putting words in His mouth; I will not dress up or down God's words. I will not soften or change what I have heard, just to pander to you!

And yet, King Balak asks for a curse for a third time, and again a blessing is spoken. For two chapters we read of the wrangling between these men because they so well know the power of words. Balak knows that words from a prophet are so powerful, so needed because they can and will change the course of a nation. He is desperate to get the words spoken to curse so that he is in the military ascendancy.

Eventually, realizing that it's never going to happen, he says in desperation, "Well if you won't curse them, then at least don't bless them!" (See Numbers 23:25.)

God does not speak in some distant way, booming from a cloud over nations. Instead He chooses to put words in the mouth of a man under pressure that shape the nation, disempower the enemy, and hold back the advances of evil men.

You are the messenger of the Lord!

Yes, you reading this: *you* are trusted with the voice of the Lord!

The words of God that come through you will create. You are a voice that enables the release of the Holy Spirit to hover and create.

You are the messenger of the Lord!

My word that goes out from my mouth: It will not return to me empty, but will accomplish what I desire and achieve the purpose for which I sent it (Isaiah 55:11).

This passage is not talking about the "Word," as in the Bible; it wasn't yet written! No, Isaiah is talking about the words of the Lord going out from a person's mouth and not returning void.

The essence of the first chapter of the Book of Jeremiah (if it has been a while since you've read Jeremiah, you really need to get back into this remarkable book) is that prophetic people will carry words that will tear down, words that will build up, words that will plant, and words will create (see Jer. 1:10). And God promises that He will watch to make sure that the words come to pass (see v. 12). He will make sure that any words from Him happen.

Is it any wonder that we have to say over our lives is what God says about us? No wonder we have to decree our miracles and then work them with words—out loud!

When you say what God says, it keeps you on course. It releases goodness. You *must* speak. You are the messenger that carries the word of the Lord for your family, your body, your nation—the word that releases the Holy Spirit to hover and to bring it forth!

If you decree the word of the Lord over your life, it opens the door to advance you.

Sometimes we need others involved in our miracles. But there are also times when your mouth needs activated and you can't just keep it in. Mirror Jesus: there were times when Jesus had to say, "Come out of that grave," "Be still, storm!" "Come out, demon!" "Be healed, blind man!" Jesus didn't just think it; He had to speak it.

Your mouth is a vehicle for the Holy Spirit to act. The issue is not about whether blindness can hear or not, or whether a dead man can hear or not; the issue is that the words can't return void. They can't return without working an effect.

> **If you decree the word of the Lord over your life, it opens the door to advance you.**

In the Lord's Prayer the stanza *"Your Kingdom come, your will be done"* is not a request; it is a command (Matt. 6:10). It is helpful to think of this phrase as saying something like, "Command the Kingdom of God to come" / "Command my Lordship over this circumstance." In fact, I believe that this line of the prayer is actually saying: "The will of the King *will* be done here; I command it!"

Step into the new territory and say, "This is the will of the King, and now it is going to happen!"

What do you need to speak out personally?

What do you need to speak out nationally?

Speak out the word of the Lord. Speak out over anti-Christ religions like Islam that Jesus is Lord. Speak out over your nation that the prodigals are coming home. Speak out over your government that they will marry righteousness. Speak out the healing of God over your family.

God is putting His words in the mouths of teenagers, and instead of cursing, they will only be able to speak blessing. They will speak the word of the Lord in their colleges, in their schools, and on their campuses; their words will be so power fused that many will come to Jesus, and the word of the Lord will be magnetic and not belittled. God will make the youth a vocal sign and wonder in these days.

Prophetic voices will be awakened amongst the student population and the voice of God will be in vogue in universities, setting a generation on fire!

The Lord says, "Students, I will visit with you like I did Moses. You will meet Me at a burning bush moment of encounter, and you will become My mouth pieces for a generation, and you will liberate them. For the spirit of Moses is falling on the late teenagers and those in their early twenties."

Right now, your mouth is being touched to speak. God is working something new in you so that you can see what God sees and say what God says. God is stirring you now to *be the voice*!

If you are willing to listen, you will hear. Don't add to it. God will give you the understanding you have been waiting on. Your mouth will be more strategic than ever before. You will find your mouth taking you places that you never thought you would go and opening doors that you never thought would open. He is giving you a massive new ability to speak on Heaven's behalf as His representative.

There is a glory in your mouth. For some of you, there are seeds in your mouth that will bring forth a great harvest; for others of you, your mouth is even on fire right now!

Now the Spirit is saying, "Pay attention to opening your mouth. Expect the word of the Lord to take over. Expect the word of the Lord to start a fire in your office."

The Lord is going to clear up your speech, and you will have clarity. God will ask you to say some things in a moment; say yes to His request immediately.

> ***You will find your mouth taking you places that you never thought you would go and opening doors that you never thought would open.***

You will release prophetic words outside the door of the church and businesspeople will start to share, even in hushed tones, that a prophetic voice turned them around. But then it will become like a domino effect and it will be *unusual* for a business to *not* have a prophet or prophetic person on a retainer contract to steer them through.

I pray for you as you read these pages, and I loose the new word of the Lord and glory speaking. Fire in your bones and coming out of your mouth! We are going to have to get used to the *fire anointing*!

ACTIVATION

When are you useful to God? What is it that makes you useful?

I believe that it is measured by how *bold* (note, not rude!) and courageous you are.

When you don't hold back.

When you refuse to say, "I won't," but instead you say, "Yes, I will, no matter what that looks like or what it takes!"

So, ask yourself, "How is my boldness and courage?"

Score yourself out of ten. Then double-check this score with God. Ask Him, "What score would You give me God?"

Do your scores match up? How do you feel about what you heard God say?

PRAYER

Father God, I'm sorry for every time that I have partnered with timidity. I reject the fear of man that has kept me quiet or silent. I want to be a bold and courageous voice for You.

Jesus, would You come and heal where my vocal cords are in retreat and make me a bold, prophetic, truth-teller. I tell the demons of silence to leave my life right now in Jesus's name, and I ask for the Holy Spirit to fill me with His holy force!

In Jesus's name, amen!

PART III

PROPHECY

171

CHAPTER 9

Essentially Spirit

Without the spiritual world the material world is a disheartening enigma.

—Joseph Joubert, French Moralist

You, however, are not in the realm of the flesh but are in the realm of the Spirit, if indeed the Spirit of God lives in you. And if anyone does not have the Spirit of Christ, they do not belong to Christ.

—Romans 8:9

YOU ARE PRIMARILY A SPIRIT

To be in any way skilled prophetically, it is important to have a grasp of some the basics of understanding the spirit realm. Let's journey through some foundational building blocks, before we consider how God speaks.

Man is essentially spirit. This must be considered as a core fundamental truth.

Man does not have a spirit inside of him. Man *is* spirit, a spirit that lives in a body. Perhaps we think of ourselves as flesh and bones, with a spirit hidden inside, but we are actually first and foremost *spirit beings*, who then have an outer shell of flesh.

When God called John to *"come up here"* (Rev. 4:1), his spirit traveled to be with God in His throne room, to interact with Him there, whilst his body remained on the earth. Just as the "flesh-man" part of you can see, hear, and relate to the material world, so your "spirit-man" can see, hear, and relate to the spiritual world, where God—who is also spirit—dwells.

There is a renewed urgency to focus on the biblical commands to engage with and be deeply aware of the spirit realm.

> *So we fix our eyes not on what is seen, but on what is unseen, since what is seen is temporary, but what is unseen is eternal* (2 Corinthians 4:18).

We have a clear scriptural mandate to focus on the unseen realm and a similar instruction is repeated in Paul's letter to the church in Colossae:

> *Set your hearts on things above, where Christ is, seated at the right hand of God. Set your minds on things above, not on earthly things* (Colossians 3:1-2).

We are to set our attention—our gaze—onto the things of Heaven, lavishing our attention on Father, Son, and Holy Spirit, right where they dwell. Ask yourself honestly how often you obey these instructions and investigate the spirit realm. How fixed is your gaze on the dimensions of the unseen? Basically, how *biblically normal* are you?

We are first and foremost spirit beings.

One day your flesh will pass away and you will become a disembodied spirit waiting for a brand-new body, but your spirit is the important part of you that remains forever.

THE IMAGE OF GOD

As we explored in an earlier chapter, God made us in His image, in His likeness, and God is spirit. We are fundamentally created spirit, like God, so that we can be intimate with Him.

The Hebrew word for image is *tselem*, which means "in the form of." Often when God is seen in Scripture, He is described as "like" a son of man, in the form of man. Every man is a spirit who came from God, *in the form of* God.

When Adam first sinned in the Garden of Eden, God appeared and asked, "*Where are you?*" (Gen. 3:9). If you were reading this passage for the very first time you might be a little bit perturbed at the concept that our supposedly all-knowing, all-seeing Creator could lose His first man! You might want to ask, "If You lost Adam so quickly, do You really know where *I* am God?"

But I don't think that God was merely giving Adam and Eve an opportunity to come out of hiding or playing some game of seek with them. What was really going on in the garden?

Every man is a spirit who came from God, in the form of God.

The three dimensions

Let's consider spirit realms and dimensions. If we lived in a 2-D (two dimensional) world, we would simply be as lines or shapes drawn on paper. Trapped in our flat, cartoonlike world, we would only be able see each other like characters in *Tom and Jerry* or a platform video game like *Space Invaders*! Our world would have no concept of depth; we would be missing that all important third dimension (3-D).

Then, imagine if one of us got bumped off that flat 2-D page and, for the first time, landed into a 3-D world! It would be mind-blowing and overwhelming to suddenly become aware of more than that original, flat world! There would be an immediate need to try to comprehend dizzyingly new concepts such as height and breadth and depth.

But what if our multidimensional traveler was then kicked back into the 2-D world? They would have the near impossible task of trying to explain their 3-D experience to an audience who'd only ever been part of a 2-D existence. They would be called crazy, delusional, unbalanced, a lunatic with no grip on reality, and perhaps forever they would grapple in vain to find the language to describe what that extra, third dimension is like to a brain that has only ever known two dimensions.

God's spirit dimension

God makes Adam out of the dust in our three dimensions, a fleshy, body image of Himself, built to survive in our three-dimensional, earthly world.

But God exists in a dimension beyond this—the spirit realm—a dimension that will blow our minds. And, as He forms Adam, our Creator does something truly remarkable. He breathes!

As God blew His breath of life into Adam's nostrils (see Gen. 2:7), He breathed His higher dimension into mankind, and we became living spirits with a spirit dimension. God gave Adam the *substance of another dimension.*

Adam's three-dimensional existence was given a heavenly dimension of *spirit* in it. God breathed in you: you are not a physical being looking for a spiritual experience. You are a spirit being having a temporary, physical experience.

> *Adam's three-dimensional existence was given a heavenly dimension of spirit in it.*

Adam could see *in the spirit.* It was perfectly normal for Adam and Eve to see God (who is, of course, spirit), strolling through the Garden of Eden in the cool of the day. This wasn't any stranger a thing to Adam than the fact that he could see, eat, and taste physical fruit in the flesh realm. But of course, as we saw earlier, Adam could also see into the *spirit realm* to know what God had intended when he made the different animals, birds, and fish. Adam had to have this other-dimensional ability, otherwise he wouldn't have been able to name the creatures correctly!

What happened at the fall?

However, everything changed at the fall. Once Adam ate the fruit, his physical eyes opened wide (*"the eyes of both of them were opened,"* Gen. 3:7), and he and Eve experienced the crippling effects of shame for the first time. Their first act was to cover up their nakedness. As Adam's spiritual eyes—his eyes into that other, heavenly dimension—began to shut, he immediately became more physically, fleshly focused. He had sinned and now he hid in shame:

> *Then the man and his wife heard the sound of the* LORD *God as he was walking in the garden in the cool of the day, and they hid from the* LORD *God among the trees of the garden. But the* LORD *God called to the man, "Where are you?"* (Genesis 3:8–9)

We always think of this verse in the sense of God promenading in the garden at that pleasant, evening, *"cool of the day"* time. But God did not come looking for them in the flesh. That word *cool* is the Hebrew word *ruach* (breath/wind/spirit). God was out looking for them in the spirit realm, where they were all used to hanging out and communing together as spirit beings.

God was not searching for Adam in our three-dimensional physical realm. He was seeking for him in the eternal, spirit realm. At the fall, Adam switched off his life in that realm and was no longer engaging in it.

> **God did not come looking for them in the flesh; He was out looking for them in the spirit realm.**

GOD STILL LOOKS FOR YOU IN THE SPIRIT REALM

In John 4 a Samaritan woman encounters Jesus by a well and asks Him where it would be appropriate for Samaritan believers to worship God—on the hill or on the mountain? Jesus's reply is, "Neither":

> *Yet a time is coming and has now come when the true worship-*
> *ers will worship the Father* **in the Spirit** *and in truth, for*
> *they are the kind of worshipers the Father seeks. God is spirit,*
> *and his worshipers must worship* **in the Spirit** *and in truth*
> (John 4:23–24).

Note Jesus's repeating of the concept of worshippers who worship *"in the spirit"* realm. God is still seeking after us! Can you feel the pain of the fall in this verse—the heartache of God still walking in the spirit and pursuing, asking and looking for those will meet Him in the spirit realm? God is hunting for us.

> **God still walks in the spirit, pursuing, asking,**
> **and looking for those who will meet**
> **Him in His spirit realm.**

You can work for God all your life, even full time as a pastor, prophet theologian, priest, or bishop—but be switched off in the spirit realm. Our work ethic can be great but our spirits dull, which is why we read:

> *Many will say to me on that day, "Lord, Lord, did we not*
> *prophesy in your name and in your name drive out demons and*
> *in your name perform many miracles?" Then I will tell them*
> *plainly, "I never knew you"* (Matthew 7:22–23).

God is known in the spirit; He is Spirit. Or to put it more bluntly, God is only truly known in the spirit realm.

The issue is that we take so much care of the physical—we wash it and clothe it—at the utter neglect of the *real us*: our spirit-man. Smith Wigglesworth said that we give our bodies three square meals, but our spirit only one meal a week, on a Sunday.[18] How can we expect to be strong enough in the battle on such a meager diet?

WHERE IS THE SPIRIT REALM?

In Scripture you often read of angels *appearing* out of the blue. We might be expecting heavenly messengers to *come down* to earth, but the spiritual realm is all around us. You need to get switched on to this, so you too can see them *appear* in an instant. We are to learn to "*fix our eyes*" where they are.

> ### God is only truly known
> ### in the spirit realm.

Either angels will appear in our physical dimension or we must learn to go into the spirit dimension that pre-fall Adam would have known. Ezekiel, Paul, John, and Daniel, for example, all went into that spiritual dimension and couldn't quite describe exactly what they saw. They had to use the tangible world to explain the intangible, using things they knew to explain things that they didn't know. John in particular expresses seeing things that are not utterable, seeing things that he could not describe. When we read about the provision of manna to the children of Israel in the wilderness (and *manna* came from the dimension of God, the very food of Heaven), the best earth-realm description we get for it is that it was like coriander seeds.

God is restoring our spiritual sight. The first thing we lost in Eden was the ability to see into the spirit realm. Now we are reclaiming it.

Elisha understood the need to navigate life through spiritual sight, to see and let it medicate your emotions, to see and let it underpin your authority. In Second Kings 6, Elijah was surrounded by Aramean enemy armies, but he was also seeing the vastness of the armies of God that also surrounded him. The reality of their presence was like a balm to him and, when his servant Gehazi finally also joined in this spiritual sight, he too came to peace, through an understanding of the higher power of the Lord who was visibly encamped around them.

> *The first thing that we lost in Eden was the ability to see into the spirit realm.*
> *Now we are reclaiming it.*

We have become trapped and limited by our unbiblical shutting down of spiritual sight. We have feared deception more than we have striven to realize that He who is in us is greater than he who is in the world (see 1 John 4:4). When it comes to the spirit realm, we have been nervous rather than excited, cynical rather than adventuring with God. Disobediently we have kept our eyes closed for safety, rather than partnering with the gift of discerning of spirits that should be what keeps us safe. (There's more on the gift of discerning of spirits in a later chapter.)

When it comes to the spirit realm, we have been nervous rather than excited, cynical rather than adventuring with God.

When we see from our usual 3-D physical dimension, we struggle with our identity. But when God takes you outside of this flesh realm and draws you into His world, you see the role and authority that you are called to function in! You taste and see His goodness firsthand and understand who you are *and whose you are*. When Jesus paid the debt for us on the cross, He enabled us to walk with God, just like Adam and Eve did—spirit to Spirit. This is the life that you are called to today. You are essentially spirit.

When I understand that I am a spirit, I don't have to expend a lot of effort to be *spiritual*, because that is what I am. This revelation should completely change how you think about connecting with God and how easy it is to do. When you get this, you will find that there is an *immediacy* to being with Him. I can immediately hear His voice, I can immediately know what God's opinion is on a matter, and I can sense His holy presence. I can know what is on Heaven's agenda today because I'm already seated in heavenly places (see Eph. 2:6), and my spirit is one with Him in Spirit (see 1 Cor. 6:17).

This is the life that you are called to today. You are essentially spirit.

If I believe that primarily I am flesh and bone who just happens to also have a spirit, it is much harder to believe that I am spiritual.

My mind will make endless conjectures, trying with incredible effort and contortions to be spiritual, but I will end up feeling frustrated. Instead we must understand that it is impossible for a spirit to *not* be spiritual! This is not to be our theology; this is to be our reality.

DECREE TIME!

Decree out loud:
"It's easy for me to be spiritual."

GOD'S GLORY THINKING

God shares Himself wholly with you.

The Old Testament word for glory is *kabod*, meaning "weight" or "heavy," indicating the thickness of God that comes to rest, pressing His fullness down upon us. However, in the New Testament the Greek word for glory is *doxa*, and this word indicates something quite remarkable: *doxa* is God's thoughts, God's opinion, God's beliefs, God's way of thinking.

God, who moves us *"from glory to glory"* (2 Cor. 3:18), tells us through the story of Scripture that He is sharing His glory—*doxa*—thinking with us in an increasing measure. And His glory gives us glory revelation, glory strategy, glory thinking, glory opinions, and glory solutions!

God has set the rules, and His rules are that we get the inside track on what God wants to say to people, the inside track on what

His opinions are about them. This is how He designed His new covenant glory to be.

In Paul's first letter to the Corinthians, he quotes the prophet Isaiah (see chapter 40:13):

> For, "Who has known the mind of the Lord so as to instruct him?"

In other words, we were in the dark. But Paul overturns this Old Testament thinking by adding:

> **But** [now] *we have the mind of Christ* (1 Corinthians 2:16).

God is not holding back His secret thoughts from you; now you have the mind of Christ!

God is sharing His glory thinking with us in an increasing measure.

God happily gives you His mind, His glory thoughts, and pulls you up to another level by His miraculous grace. We all face life situations that require God's thinking rather than our own, but thankfully He has chosen to liberally share His opinion with His children. Yes, there is a secret wisdom of the Kingdom, there are great mysteries to be discovered, but we, miraculously, have the mind of Christ and can access them.

God's glory changes our perspective.

When you are atop a high building, things look very different than at ground level. On a mountain summit, things are different again. Then, from out of an airplane's window you have an almost unrecognizably different reality—you see a bigger picture. When you come into the Kingdom of God, you come into His reality. You go higher than an airplane and get to see with the glory reality of Heaven. You get the perspective and opinion of God on a matter.

God is calling us to understand the deep things of His Kingdom, the things of His Heaven, and to partner with what He is doing. He calls us to enter into spiritual sight, deep levels of Him and of prophetic revelation that we never dreamed or imagined!

Paul reinforces this truth a second time, this time quoting from Isaiah 64:4:

> *"What no eye has seen, what no ear has heard, and what no human mind has conceived"–the things God has prepared for those who love him–*[but] *these are the things God has revealed to us by his Spirit* (1 Corinthians 2:9–10).

God says here through Paul, "I want to show you what I have prepared for the future." We lean into this biblical truth again and again as we prophesy.

When you come into the Kingdom you get the perspective and opinion of God on a matter.

Seated in heavenly places

We are seated in heavenly places, in the third Heaven, where God has His throne.

And God raised us up with Christ and seated us with him in
the heavenly realms in Christ Jesus (Ephesians 2:6).

Have you seen the seat you already have in Heaven yet? God doesn't just offer you a place in front of Him where you worship. Instead He places you in a chair of co-reigning and co-laboring with Him. (Though, like the twenty-four elders, I expect that we'll be off our seats and casting down our crowns!) Nevertheless, the seat that you have is a forward-facing, ruling location.

There is a big difference between knowing this positionally and intellectually on the one hand and then understanding it relationally, where it is practically applied, on the other. But when you can apply this truth and have it marinade inside of you, it builds in you the understanding that you have access to God and the ways of Heaven.

God is on the throne, Jesus is at His right hand, and you sit with them.

You don't have to strain very hard to hear the business of Heaven. You are not on the outer courts. You are seated at the center with your Father and your Savior. Applying this truth opens you up to understand the spiritual realm. You are not fighting for access; you *have* access. It enables you to enter the most beautiful places in the dimensions of the spirit. Then you can see God face to face and hear His voice with real clarity—not when you die but here, now. You just need to believe it!

> **You are not fighting for access to**
> **the spiritual realm, you *have* access.**

TOP TIP

Sometimes all you need to say before you prophesy is, "I'm seated with You, Jesus." At this you remind your spirit to become aware of God's communication that is right with you.

Every day, when you wake up, why not make the declaration, "I'm seated in heavenly places. What is Heaven doing today, God?"

Then make this kind of conversation a habit.

PERSONAL NAVIGATION OF THE SPIRIT REALM

Before ministering to others as a prophetic warrior, seeing and hearing what God has for them, there is a need to navigate the spirit realm as a fighter. This is so that you know how to be free yourself. We must know freedom in order to minister freedom.

Let's spend the next pages gaining an understanding of the prophetic warrior mindset that you need to have over yourself, and what that looks like in the spiritual realm.

Accepting what is already approved

If you are Christian believer, God has made an everlasting covenant with you. He has covenanted with your born-again, new identity. Therefore, He doesn't see you as you were in the past; He sees you as Jesus. Jesus died *for* you, and He died *as* you.

If Jesus had only been looking to change your behavior a little bit, if it had only been behavior modification in you that He wanted, for you to act better, then Jesus did not need to die.

At the point of your salvation your "old man" (who you were) died and you became a new creation. From that point onward, God saw you and sees you as righteous, continuously and forevermore.

> *God made him who had no sin to be sin for us, so that **in him we might become the righteousness of God*** (2 Corinthians 5:21).

Why would you then spend the rest of your life waiting for God to move on you, when He is already in you? What possible moment are you waiting for that could be as epic as the one when Jesus took up residence inside you and made you His home?

Rather, the Spirit of God is seeking to spring up and overwhelm you from the inside out, where He and you are already one!

You see, we seem to spend a lot of time in our churches saying and singing things like, "Come, Holy Spirit." But "Come, Holy Spirit" is really an old covenant, Old Testament thought.

There is a danger that, the more we say, "Come, Holy Spirit," the more we strap the wrong thinking to our minds and make ourselves believe that we are somehow not yet ready, not worthy, not likable, not holy enough, not hosting-the-Spirit-of-God-already enough inside us. If we're not careful, we can adopt the resulting mindset that we are only spiritually validated when the Holy Spirit comes and makes us shake or fall over or feel the hairs on our neck stand up! Be aware that the language of the Kingdom of God can often conflict with the language of church tradition!

"Come, Holy Spirit" is really an Old Testament thought.

God sees you as righteous. He sees where He is going to explode up from within the depths of you.

The issue is that we are looking for approval, but we are *already* approved. Instead of waiting with eyes closed and arms outstretched for His approval, we need to move into *accepting* what is already approved!

God says to you today, "I want you to feel secure in My acceptance."

So, if you are used to saying, "Come, Holy Spirit" in ministry, why not try something like, "Holy Spirit explode within us today!" or "Take over all of us from the inside out!" instead?

The old man is dead

Because God has made you new and sees you as Jesus, He is *never* thinking about your "old man," who you were. He is dead! Father God is not talking to Jesus, rolling His eyes, and worrying about your old man—*he is dead!* Instead He is talking your "new man" into something. He is talking you into something spectacular, something as outrageous today as a new creation!

To always focus on how sinful or awful you are denies the fullness of what Jesus did on the cross for you. God is not interested in rehashing old conversations about how you used to be. And when we repent, He puts your sin *"as far as the east is from the west"* (Ps. 103:12). Therefore, when you keep bringing it all up again, God replies incredulously, "What are you talking about? I've chosen to forget all about that. That is not who you are to Me!"

You are not wrestling against your flesh. You have an old nature, and that old nature God did not fix—He killed it. God did not repair you; He killed you! The repetition through Romans chapters 5 to 7 on unpacking how dead you actually are is like a machine gun, sending off volleys of truth to hit you in the head, over and over again. You are *dead, dead, dead*!

Let me go over this once more, for extreme clarity: God is not restoring your old man. He is not fixing your old man. He already annihilated it. He made you a new creation. No longer are you classed as a sinner.

> *Therefore, if anyone is in Christ, the new creation has come: The old has gone, the new is here!* (2 Corinthians 5:17)

The battleground of the mind

Do you ever find yourself saying something like, "I'm wrestling with my thoughts" or "I'm battling against my flesh"? If so, it's time to stop it. You're not! You are wrestling against *someone* who wants to make you think that you are wresting against yourself. Why? Because if the deceiver can make you believe that the fight is with yourself then he knows that you have no antidote to that.

Remember, the thing you are wrestling with has no authority over you unless you give it to him. The battleground is in your mind.

God is not restoring your old man. He is not fixing your old man. He already annihilated it. He made you a new creation.

The way that you know you are in a battle is because you are wrestling thoughts, but your thoughts are *not* the battle. *The thoughts that you have are the weapons that are used against you.*

The thoughts that trouble you are being sent as bullets from outside you. If you are in a war, you do not spend all your time trying to fire at the bullets! No! You fire at the person who sent the bullets. You kill the enemy, rather than try to catch his ammunition in your hands.

Your battle is in the spirit realm. You are fighting with spirits that are against you.

Some days are real battle days, when we find ourselves thinking the thoughts the enemy has fired at us. It is vitally important that we don't pick up the enemy's bullets and bombs and take them on board.

> *The battle is not for your mind, although the battleground is in your mind. Your thoughts are **not** the battle. The thoughts that you have are the **weapons** that are used against you.*

Some days you will need worship music on all day and no TV, just because you know it's a battle day. Those are the days when the enemy is trying to make you own thoughts such as "you are going you die," "you are worthless," "you need to kill yourself," or "you are going to do something crazy."

And on these days you will have to say, "You are a lying spirit, and I am not going to listen to you. I am going to put my determination into not letting you win."

These sorts of battle days appear when you are at the point of greatest advancing. They come when you are going through the most important doors of your life, and the enemy sends a volley of shots because of your progressing position.

Fighting in the spirit realm

As I travel the world, I am continually shocked by how low our understanding of the spiritual realm is, even amongst many of us who are supposed to be the cutting-edge ones who model partnership with the Holy Spirit.

We read that our wrestle is *not* against flesh and blood, but against spiritual forces (see Eph. 6:12). But then we spend our lives beating ourselves up rather than beating the enemy up or, worse, beating other people up rather than the enemy. We get so caught up in the physical life!

When we read *"pray in the Spirit"* (Eph 6:18), we think that this means "pray in tongues," but that's not what it says (though glossolalia can be one application of this). The verse plainly says, *"pray **in the Spirit**."* In other words, pray according to the spirit realm. Pray by what you have seen in the spirit; go into the spirit realm and do business. The word *in* matters here. Just as you are probably *in* a room reading this, so you must go in to the rooms of the spirit realm to pray. Put on the lens of spiritual sight.

The same concept in seen in Jude's letter: *"building yourselves up in your most holy faith and praying in the Holy Spirit"* (Jude 20). Hence why we read, as discussed earlier, *"so we fix our eyes not on what is seen, but on what is unseen"* (2 Cor. 4:18).

Pray by what you have seen in the spirit; go into the spirit realm and do business.

We go into the spirit realm; we find the offensive demon that is attacking us, and we fight until the head of the demon that is sending the bullets falls off. We see it; we hear the *thud* on the floor, and we know the battle is over. We pray knowing when we have won, and we change our prayers, not wearing ourselves out because we're not sure if the job is done yet!

We fight in another dimension. We have already learned how to survive, fight, pull no punches, and negotiate in the flesh, now it's a necessity to learn this in the spirit. This is how we were made to function. Remember, we were made to live in the spirit realm. We were made to flow with God as He moves. It is time for you to have stories to tell of what you did in the spiritual realm!

For example, consider an anger problem. In the old man we don't realize there is a spiritual battle going on and so we relegate the blame to a problem with our flesh or our mind. We spend all our time trying to counsel ourselves out of something that we need to kill. Therefore, our efforts to deal with our anger problem become all about anger management.

Conversely, in the new man we are born into the Spirit, born by the Spirit. Our spirit is one with the Spirit of God. Therefore, anger is broken off by using our authority in the spirit realm to say, "I bring down my sword of the Spirit and break that chain of anger that a demon has placed around me."

Born to destroy!

We are born to destroy—destroy the works of the devil, just as Jesus did. So, when the enemy says to you, "I'm going to kill you" and you feel completely overwhelmed with anxiety and negative thoughts, you should turn around to him and say: "No! *I* am going to kill *you*! It's what I was born to do!"

After all, if a thief comes to raid your house and you catch him in the act, you don't sit down and let him carry on. Definitely not! Tell any demon that tries to harass or oppress you, "If you come to my house, I am going to take you out!"

Don't let the devil attack your confidence.

Never forget that satan fears Jesus. He fears His methods, His will, His ways, and His people. That's right; satan fears prophetic warriors who know who they are in the spirit!

Satan's aim is therefore to go after and destroy your confidence, which reduces your ability to use the weapons that you have that are way more powerful than his. He knows that if you raise your sword, he's dead, so he will try to convince you that you don't have the strength to do it.

What happens is that satan or one of his minions will give you a thought and, if we're not spiritually minded enough, we'll not even recognize that it's not even our thought! We begin to think to ourselves, "How could I even think this?" The demon then builds on this, "Oh, look at that terrible thought; you are evil. How could God ever love you?" If you don't shut him up, he'll keep on whispering in your ear, "You call yourself a Christian? You go to church, but look at what is going on behind your mask...."

He is called the accuser of the brethren for a reason. Be on your guard against his schemes.

JESUS RAIDS HADES

Do you ever wonder what it must have been like after Jesus was killed and become a disembodied spirit, before receiving His resurrection body? We know that He went down to the realm of the dead to get the keys of death, hell, and the grave. Using these, He locked up the power of death and the grave forevermore!

Following His death for our sin, Jesus journeyed to hades (the city of death), the realm of satan. On His way He liberated Abraham, Isaac, Jacob, David, John the Baptist, and the rest of the Old Testament faithful (those who had died righteous), ransoming them from the power of hades/sheol. We know from Ephesians that they ascended with Him back to His realm: "*When he ascended on high, he took many captives and gave gifts to his people*" (Eph. 4:8).

I don't think for a second that Jesus waked into hades, ducking and diving and hiding behind Archangel Michael, whilst He worked out a secretive stealth plan. I doubt that he sat down for hours beforehand with His angel armies, poring over a map of the city for hours so that they could form a multipronged approach in case one of them was caught off guard.

No! This is the moment of the terrorizing of darkness. This is the moment that all of Heaven has waited and longed for. This is the moment satan would have feared more than anything, though he was most likely completely blindsided by what was happening. Just a few moments before, when Jesus had breathed His last, satan was probably cracking open the champagne, thinking that *he* had won.

I image that every principality and power for good or evil turned and watched in the spirit realm to see what Jesus's spirit would do after it left His body!

I cannot image it was anything other than glorious when Jesus strode right up to the very door of darkness, His eyes blazing like fire, burning up all that was evil. If "*mountains melt like wax before the LORD*" (Ps. 97:5), would death not also melt away before Him.

No demon can stand, and no demon can move. Jesus walked right up to satan's most prized wall, the wall where he hangs his keys. He would have simply reached out His hand, unopposed, and, with no hindrance, shouted, "Mine!" before taking the keys back!

Then, with every demon pinned to the ground by the very holiness that emanates from Jesus, He started preaching in the very home of depravity itself. Probably, at this very moment every demon in hades suddenly gets a dawning understanding of the master plan of salvation that has just unfolded. Was it also at this moment that satan realized that he had failed?

Jesus would have walked out of there just as easily as He walked in, except that this time He was coming with all the captives of death who were righteous.

> *And having disarmed the powers and authorities, he made a public spectacle of them, triumphing over them by the cross* (Colossians 2:15).

Have you ever asked Jesus to show you what He saw when He terrorized darkness? Have you asked Him to show you a postcard image of that moment?! I think that if we were to see it all play out, then perhaps we would grasp hold of how to stop being impressed (or overwhelmed) with all that darkness tries to do and say to us.

> *For this purpose the Son of God was manifested, that he might destroy the works of the devil* (1 John 3:8 NKJV).

The devil is a withering branch. He has been cut off from the source of life, and he is in continual decay. End your partnership with being impressed by him.

New territory

You can destroy hell with the Heaven that is inside of you! This is how you must think from now on.

Most of the intense battles that happen in or around our life start when we enter new territory—our promised land, land that we have not yet begun to inhabit.

God is asking you to open your spiritual eyes and see what the new territory is that God has for you.

Upon opening your eyes, suddenly you will realize that evil spirits have been resisting you and keeping you out of fullness. There is a waking up that needs to happen to the spiritual conflict that is around some of the things that you are called to do.

If you have had some low moments recently, may I suggest that it could be a demon resisting you that *you* are supposed to deal with. In the spirit, the presence of evil wants to resist you, and that's why we wrestle—the enemy is trying stop your pursuit of destiny.

> *God is asking you to open your spiritual eyes and see what the new territory is that God has for you.*

God says to you: "Come and see! See the greatness that I have bestowed on you. See in the spirit and I will train your hands to win the battle. See in Heaven that everyone is celebrated for who they are and *not* for what they are not. Come and see over nations; see blueprints and maps for the future. See how Heaven conducts business; see My finger pointing to the place where you will have your next miracle. See where to move and how to raise the finances."

PRAYER

Father God, change my dullness and my low-grade ability to fight, so that I might partner with You from today. God, challenge me where I am stale, shake me where I am religious, expand me where I am small.

Jesus, I want to see into the spirit realm and to pray in the spirit as You have commanded. Open my eyes that I might see! Jesus, I repent for any time that I, or anyone in my family line, has opened wrong pathways to spiritual sight that has caused me to fear and has polluted my sight. I am sorry and, in the name of Jesus, I now command shut all wrongly opened doors!

Holy Spirit, I want to see all that You have for me and to have a clear sight so that I can be victorious in battle! Help me to live unimpressed by satan and in obedient, courageous response to the Father.

In Jesus's name, amen!

A BLESSING

As one who sees in the spirit, I loose the biblical blessing of spiritual sight over you right now. I command dullness of sight to fall away! I release strength to your inner man to keep short accounts in the spirit realm, even as you see the enemy and overcome. In Jesus's name!

CHAPTER 10

How God Speaks

The difference between the right word and the almost right word is the difference between lightning and a lightning bug.

—Mark Twain

The voice of the LORD strikes with flashes of lightning.

—Psalm 29:7

ALL SENSES ALIVE

God is communicating all the time; our job is to learn to discern it. He does not announce, "Excuse me, I about to speak, are You ready to receive?" God is not human, His first language is not English, and His accent is not even Northern Irish, like mine! We have the responsibility to learn *His* language.

When I call David on the phone, I don't say, "It's Emma your wife calling, the one you married twenty-one years ago." All I need to say is, "Hi." He knows my voice and how I sound. He even knows from how I'm breathing what sort of conversation we are going to have. Similarly, with God, we must learn what He sounds like to us and His ways of communicating—His facial expressions, how He uses nature to speak, His breath, His movements, His body language, and, of course, His voice.

When you are switched on to the Holy Spirit, it impacts and even invades all your senses. Hebrews 5 contains an outlandish Scripture that we must contend with: *"But solid food is for the mature, who because of practice have their senses trained to discern good and evil"* (Heb. 5:14 NASB). When we read *"solid food is for the mature,"* we all want to jump up and down and say, "Yes, please to solid food!" and, "Yes, please to maturity!"

But how do you get this solid food? It is not by measuring your church attendance or by going to Bible college or by your piety. It is by *training your senses.* This is totally opposite to everything that those of us who were raised in traditional churches were taught. Traditional and religious church life trained us to keep our emotions shut down and discipled us that "sensing" is dubious at best and downright dangerous at worst. The Western evangelical Church has tended to value academic rhetoric over encounter and invests everything in training our heads rather than training our senses. Yet we read here in Hebrews that biblical maturity is measured in how well you train your senses! When your senses are alive to feel, taste, touch, and experience God, *then* you are mature. *Then* you know what is good and what is evil.

God is "sense" orientated. He is wired to feel and experience us as friends.

I have trained my children's senses to know what love is like. My children know that I love them because I write it down for them: notes left in bedrooms; Valentine's cards; over-the-top lavish words written in birthday cards, which they keep safe for years. These are penned stories of love, lifelong records.

> *Biblical maturity is measured in*
> *how well you trained your senses.*

They also know the *look* of love, a facial expression that wrinkles in tenderness, smiles and bends toward them. My children know the *touch* of love—from a fierce embrace to kisses all over, tickles at bedtime, and dances in the kitchen. The *sounds* of love are present in their lives through pet names and words that wash a heart and keep it secure with language that anchors in acceptance, no matter what.

They even know the *smell* of love, for example, the scent of my favorite perfume hanging in the air, triggering their olfactory nerves. When they were little I would jokingly call from another room, "Children! I smell naughtiness in the spirit. What are you up to?" (I think all mothers have this prophetic ability!) Now that they are older, when the same call goes out the reply is usually, "Mummy, we are going to test you as a prophet. What sort of naughtiness do you smell?" And my children certainly know the *taste* of love, especially when I cook their favorite requests, like mac and cheese. They love the time and effort given to create their top picks.

These senses we switch on and train in the spirit. God wants to encounter us as a loving father, and so what does it mean to train your senses to know what is God and what is not God?

Have you ever *smelled* the perfume of Jesus? Psalm 45:8 lists His fragrance as myrrh, aloes, and cassia (a little like Christmas scents, appropriately enough, cinnamon-like). When Jesus walks into a room, this is what your spirit should smell. God's breath in Song of Songs chapter 7 is described as apple scented. So, when God breathes on you, you might smell sweet apples. Perhaps this was the first smell that Adam ever had when God blew him to life? (If it was, isn't it little wonder that satan used an apple to corrupt Adam and Eve?)

We *"taste and see that the LORD is good"* (Ps. 34:8). And our Communion sacrament is loaded with the sensory language of "eating" and "drinking" Jesus's body and blood. Our ears are made to hear His voice. John explains that the Good Shepherd's *"sheep listen to my voice"* (John 10:27).

Consider the beauty of Ephesians 2, God *"made us alive in Christ"* (Eph. 2:5; see also Col. 2:13; 1 Cor. 15:22). It would be well worth our time if we were to meditate on what *being fully alive* actually means for our senses, both natural and spiritual! We are only scraping the surface in these few paragraphs. There are even greater dimensions of God and greater encounters to be had in the biblical road to maturity.

In the rest of this chapter we will journey together through a list of the ways that God communicates, in order to put some meat on the bones of answering the question, "What is biblically 'normal' in a supernatural lifestyle?" Do keep a check list as we go. If one way of communication is familiar to you and you already interact with God at that level, give Him thanks and ask for a deeper encounter in this area. If you have *never* experienced something on the list, then why not ask God to take you by the hand and lead you into new revelatory waters?

1. Spiritual perception

The starting point on many people's prophetic journeys does not usually involve seeing or hearing. It simply involves sensing something. So you might say, "I sensed" or "I felt." Spiritual perception is in the realm of "just knowing," or of an impression. For example, have you ever heard someone say, "I have the impression that God wants me to…"?

The Holy Spirit might reveal something to you by a nudge. You might not be able to describe it in a picture, but you have a hunch, a gut feeling, or a prompting. Perhaps you feel something that you can't quite explain but it is due to a Holy Spirit push inside of you. As much as this spiritual sense seems so small and vague, it is our start point, and we do not despise the day of small beginnings! (See Zech. 4:10.) Many prophets know how to navigate these hunches and bring remarkably accurate words from them.

Mind where you park!

We used to live on a very steep hill and always parked our car on the street outside our terraced home, which was halfway down the hill. One evening, as I was driving back from work, I felt a nudge in my spirit to park at the top of the hill and walk down the hill. It was certainly not a booming voice or even a conversation with God. I simply had a feeling and knew to be obedient to that.

That night as we slept, the handbrake of the car parked in front of ours failed. The car rolled down the hill, gaining speed and zig-zagging across the street like a pinball before coming to rest in our neighbor's garden. The car's slalom wrecked every vehicle in the street—apart from ours, which stood alone, untouched, at the top of the hill.

Do you ever have these spiritual perceptions? If yes, "Hallelu-jah!" You are on the prophetic road and are already moving in tune with the Holy Spirit. If not, ask the Holy Spirit to give you a sensitization to Him.

ACTIVATION

PRACTICING YOUR
SPIRITUAL PERCEPTION

Ask God to give you an impression, a nudge, or a knowing about something that He wants you to do in your own life. It could be very simple such as calling a friend, getting more exercise, or buying flowers for someone. Allow a sense from God to grow in you about an action you need to take.

2. Pictorial visions

Pictorial visions are Holy Spirit visual aids. We see them with our inner sight and then tell others about "getting a picture," in other words, a still, nonmoving image. From clocks to trees, candlesticks to tripods, God will often pick a vision that means something deeply significant to the person that you are ministering to.

I once saw mushrooms midway through giving a prophetic word to a woman, and on enquiring of her, discovered that she had a severe allergy to them. God had illustrated a warning about something that the woman was not to touch through a relatable picture that clearly made His point and would not be easy to forget.

It is very important to ask what the Holy Spirit's interpretation of your picture is and not *assume* an interpretation. What a dog, for example, might mean to you may well not be what the Holy Spirit is saying; you might *hate* dogs, but God might be speaking of loyalty.

Sometimes you might see a semitransparent picture, superimposed over the person you are looking at and prophesying over.

One of my team members would regularly see words written on a person's forehead, and these would reveal what is dominating that person's mind.

Another team member's son, who was too young to have any anatomical understanding, would see parts of people's bodies turn black as he looked at them. He would know in the spirit that they were carrying an illness in that area or organ. During prayer he would see the black turn green as Jesus healed the person.

With pictorial visions you will standardly hear someone saying phrases like, "The Lord is showing me," "I am seeing," or "Does this picture mean anything to you?"

TOP TIP

If the picture you receive seems strange, go with it! Enjoy lingering with God.

One night I was up in the middle of the night, feeding one of the children. I was totally sleep deprived, but as I sat there, a friend appeared in my mind and morphed into a chocolate from a box, a very soft chocolate-covered caramel with a hard hazelnut in its center! God urged me to muse on this picture and then said, *"She thinks she is soft and fragile and will easily be destroyed, but in her center is a strong solidity, like the nut within the caramel."*

I did think this was a bit ridiculous until He said, "I have a scripture to back this picture up."

"Really God?"

But sure enough, the Holy Spirit reminded me, *"We are hard pressed on every side, but not crushed* (2 Cor. 4:8). She and I have never forgotten this picture, and years later, even in harder times for her, the truth is well planted. All because of a late-night chocolate picture!

The Bible is packed full of accounts of prophets seeing pictorial visions. God and Jeremiah have a few strategic interactions over pictures:

"What do you see Jeremiah?"

"I see a boiling pot, tilting from the north" – or, "I see the branch of an almond tree."[19]

Both of these relatively simple pictures became the foundations for important national words that have been recorded for posterity in Holy Scripture.

> **The Bible is packed full of accounts of prophets seeing pictorial visions.**

3. Closed panoramic visions

A "closed panoramic vision" sounds very grand but, simply put, this is when the picture you see begins to move, rather like a DVD film playing in your mind.

Act 9 records Ananias receiving a vision that he is to go and lay hands on Saul (later Paul) so that he might receive his sight back. In his vision Ananias was told that Saul had also had a vision of what would happen. These visions built the trust that was required for a very important encounter between Ananias and Saul to take place.

A closed panoramic vision is usually "seen" with eyes closed. You have an internal moving vison, through inner sight, which means the Holy Spirit projects the image into your mind.

I train my staff *not* to do this with closed eyes in ministry as it is best practice to prophesy to someone with your eyes open. This is so that you can be fully aware of all that is happening to them. This is called an open panoramic vision.

4. Open panoramic visions

As above, but this time when you see a heavenly DVD being played out, *your eyes are open.* Nevertheless, an open panoramic vision it still usually something you see playing in your mind, like the Holy Spirit is shining a film projector into your mind.

5. Seeing in the spirit

This aspect of the supernatural gifts of God is often referred to as "having a seer's gift" or a "seer ability" (as in "see-er"—someone who sees). This is where the "veil" between the natural and spiritual realm is either very thin or is removed altogether and you can see what is happening in both realms. In Scripture, Samuel is called both a prophet *and* a seer and in the courts of King David we find both Nathan the prophet and Gad the seer:

> *As for the events of King David's reign, from beginning to end, they are written in the records of Samuel the seer, the records of Nathan the prophet and the records of Gad the seer* (1 Chronicles 29:29).

The word we translate as seer, *chozeh,* is from the Hebrew *chazah,* meaning to see, to behold, to become aware, to become visible. It also means to experience.

Feeling, sensing, seeing, and experiencing are huge parts of a seer's life. Those who operate in this gift a lot tend to love extended times of worship, and they enjoy immensely the encounters that it opens up to them. Those who are predominately seer-oriented, *feel* their revelation. It is a sense-based revelation and often produces a sense-based response. They feel *deeply* and *urgently* about their encounters! Jeremiah the seer prophet describes the feeling of revelation in extreme ways like fire in his bones (see Jer. 20:9).

You can very quickly tell which biblical prophets are seers because of the descriptive and image-laden language they use when writing. Ezekiel is a prime example, with his describing of *wheels within wheels*, and visions of God seated on the throne outside the center of the earth. God coaches Jeremiah according to his seer gift, asking him on several occasions, "What do you see?" each time expecting Jeremiah to look again more intently at what God is revealing. In Isaiah's prophesy you can almost hear the sound of the whip lashing the back of Jesus, seven hundred years before His torture at the hands of Roman soldiers. Such is the impact of Isaiah's image-laden prophecy, *"by His stripes we are healed"* (Isaiah 53:5 NKJV).

The wonderful strength of the seer is the power of the images released from them to people, as well as the feelings and responses they create in people to God. A potential weakness to watch out in seers is that they can get too emotive and overemotional. A seer carries the potential to get bogged down in the detail of images that are of no real use or relevance to others beyond the seer, or in images that others find strange and upsetting. Sadly, this has often led to a heartbreaking struggle for acceptance in the church or society, not necessarily through any fault of the seers themselves.

In our Glasgow center we help our seers with this by making them practice getting a picture and then *not* mentioning the picture when they prophesy. All they do is use the picture or vision as an internal trigger to bring forth the word of the Lord.

The real joy of this aspect of our Christian life is it can be switched on in an instant, even if your spiritual eyes have been closed up until now, just as it did for Elisha's servant Gehazi.[20] Having your spiritual eyes opened will reveal where there are the angels in the room, or which mantle is sitting on a person, or which demonic hindrances are present in a place. One of my life's greatest joys is seeing and encountering in the spiritual realm. On a public platform I tend to gush forth with lots of words, but in the private place this is how I meet God.

I once heard a UK prophet who has since passed to glory outline a season in their life where God totally removed the barrier between the natural and the spiritual realms. He spoke of almost losing his mind because of how intense the experience was. He reported seeing and hearing people's pain and emotions coming off them as colors. This type of experience made obsolete any low-grade questions we might ask of the spirit realm like, "Can a demon read your mind?" (The answer is no.) The "reality" is that we exude (give off) so much in the spirit that it is relatively straightforward for spiritual beings, or those who see in the spirit, to watch what is happening with us. The elder prophet outlined fear as being a particularly strong *sound* and that he could hear it for up to a five-mile radius coming off people, which made it very challenging for him to sleep at all during that period.

> *Having your spiritual eyes opened will reveal where there are the angels in the room, or which mantle is sitting on a person, or which demonic hindrances are present in a place.*

Now, I appreciate that very few of us may experience something quite as intense as this, however, here are some stories of my family's day-to-day life as seers.

Where is Jesus in your bedroom?

At bedtime when they were very small, I would ask my children to tell me where Jesus was in their bedroom. I made this a rigorous question I asked every night, deliberately training them to look and see but to only see Jesus so that they would orient to Him, first and always. This establishes the pattern in our children for their rest of their lives that we look at Him, no matter what. Jesus modeled this in His own life; He looked, and He only did what He saw the Father do. Jesus was seeing and paying attention and orienting Himself to the work of God and God only.

Some evenings the children would tell me that Jesus was wearing pajamas. At first this had me a little theologically concerned (because Jesus *never slumbers or sleeps* [see Ps. 121:4]) and I would question them about this. "Oh Mummy!" they would sigh with mock exasperation, "Jesus is just coming to give me a cuddle before I sleep!"

> *I deliberately trained them to look and see but to only see Jesus so that they would orient to Him, first and always.*

Other times Jesus would show Himself to them in military clothes, and they would chat about a battle that He was going to help them win. Or in fisherman's clothing...conversations about souls getting saved would follow. Sometimes Jesus would simply be in a dancing mood and just having fun.

Out of the mouths of babes

Over time, seeing in the spirit became each child's own personal journey, and they would come to me, asking questions like, "Why are all the angels in this shopping mall crying?"

On another occasion, one of the boys said to me, "I can see a dinosaur-like demon in this soft play area. He's hiding to scare all the children in the dark corner." I equipped them with simple prayers that they could use to pray and clear rooms of demonic interference, for the well-being of others.

Massage prayer in the playground

One day my daughter Jessica came to me, aged 11, and asked if she could give me a massage.

"But you don't know how to massage!" I said to her.

"I do," she retorted. "Jesus taught me."

"When did this happen?" I asked.

"Mummy, I heard you teach about the laying on of hands and so I asked Jesus how I could lay hands on my friends in school to help them find Him. He told me to get them to lie down on the playground at lunchtime, in groups of three. I looked into the Spirit realm and I put my hands where I saw Jesus put His hands, and He taught me to massage as I prayed and then all my friends got to know Jesus!"

A child's sight unlocked church victory

When our middle child, Peter, was still in diapers, he would spend a lot of time in the creche area (for babies and toddlers) of the churches we visited. On one occasion I was in a large church, and Peter came to tell me that there were spiders in the creche. He was insistent, and so I asked whether they were real or demonic (an important question!). He confirmed that, yes, they were demonic spiders. Having already trained him in simple warfare prayers, I asked why he hadn't already told them to, "Go away in Jesus's name" and, bless him, he said that he'd tried but that they *just wouldn't go.* Well, at this, my interest was piqued, my protective mothering instinct was in overdrive, my discernment was "on," and I just had to go and investigate!

As I marched into the baby room, I could see (in the spirit) a large sexual perversion demon living in the corner of the creche, with lesser-sized demons coming off him. Gross! It was these lesser-sized demons that the Holy Spirit had shown Peter as spiders.

Although I was furious to see this gross sight sitting amongst our precious babies and toddlers, I paused to ask God for *His* strategy to approach and deal with the problem. A demonic spirit like this, which had been in place for some time and couldn't be easily shifted, would have had to have been given permission (by someone with authority) to be in that place. I recognized that, because I did not have the authority over that place, any warfare that I would have done would have only postponed the problem, or possibly made things worse.

I therefore approached the pastor of that church—with a fair degree of trepidation to be honest—knowing that he had no grid of reference for what I was about to say to him!

"You have a large demon of sexual perversion in the children's area, and he is throwing his weapons at your church. I expect that you must have a higher proportion of pornography, adultery, and sexual sin in this church than would be normal."

The pastor agreed and told me that he had been working hard to help an inordinate number of struggling people and couples in his church.

"That demon has some permission to be here. What happened in leadership that was not dealt with that is giving it access?" I asked.

It transpired that, some time ago, there had been someone in leadership in that church who had been downloading sexually explicit images onto his church computer. Although it had been discovered, the issue had been largely "brushed under the carpet." Since that time, the church had been remodeled, and where Peter and I had seen the demon in the creche was formerly the site of where that leader's desk had been!

The pastor repented for not dealing effectively with the former leader's sin, and because he had authority in the situation, we were able to kick the demon out. Praise God, the pastor later reported an immediate healing in many lives that had been ravaged by sexual sin. All because a tiny child saw in the spirit!

A sibling's guardian angel

We have some conversations in our home that are everyday to us, but I guess some people might find them a little strange. Jessica will tell me that her guardian angel is sometimes the only one who laughs at her jokes!

One day she happened to remark, in passing, that she had seen an angel on our stairs.

When I asked her to describe the angel, I realized that I recognized it.

"Jessica, that's your little brother's angel!"

"Oh yeah," she replied, realizing that she had talked herself into trouble.

"Jessica, what were you doing to your brother that meant that his guardian angel had to give you a hard stare?"

Sheepishly, she confessed to me that they had been fighting.

ACTIVATION

If spiritual sight is something that you wish to pursue, it takes practice. I suggest that you ask the question, "Where is Jesus in the room?" on a regular basis. Ask the Holy Spirit to open your eyes to see Him. Look and see what colors He is wearing, for example. What clothes is He wearing? What emotions are coming off Him for you? Does He have anything to give you? What is His facial expression?

We have businesspeople who do this in their marketplace offices on a regular basis.

Ask: "Jesus, who are You standing next to in this office? That is where I need to stand because that is where there will be a breakthrough!"

Ask: "Jesus, whose house in my street are You standing outside of? That is the house that I need to go and knock on the door. If You are there, I want to be there too."

6. Dreams

A dream is a visionary revelation that you receive whilst asleep. (But you probably already knew that!) Of course, Daniel and Joseph are our biblical experts when it comes to dreams and dream interpretation.

God *always* wants to speak to us, but often during the day He can hardly get a word in edgewise! However, when we are asleep, our souls become more rested and we are more inclined to receive from Him. He bypasses our analytical minds and patiently downloads what we need in our sleep. Thank God that He is so persistent with us! Rather than giving up on us, He waits until we are asleep, comes quietly in the night, and says, "I want to talk to you."

> **"Jesus, who are you standing next to in this office? That is where I need to stand because that is where there will be a breakthrough!"**

It is useful to have a "dream journal" by your bed because it is easy to forget them later in the day. I also suggest that you invest in a good Bible-based dream interpretation dictionary to assist your understanding.

TOP TIP

Before you open your eyes in the morning, ask: *"Jesus, is there a dream You need me to remember from the night before?"* Go over the details with Jesus to anchor them in your memory and then open your eyes. If you don't recall anything, ask Jesus to help your spirit remember the lessons He taught you in the night, even as your flesh has forgotten.

Many prophetic people prophesy over others from their dreams as standard practice. I have found dreams to be incredibly emotionally healing. Jesus hides in the night and presents Himself to me in ways that I can work with. I often wake up emotionally in a different place from how I went to sleep. My whole inner being has been ministered to by revelation. Jesus knows how I'm wired and exactly what is needed.

I believe that as a body we need to prepare for the mass interpretation of dreams. Thousands are going to dream as the Holy Spirit is poured out, just as Joel prophesied.[21]

Perhaps it is time to train in dream interpretation so that you can then offer this at your church. Dreams are how many are going to come to faith in these days. Many thousands of Muslims around the world are already meeting Jesus in their dreams in miraculous ways. It's time to ask for the children in our secular nations to meet Jesus in their dreams as well. I recently heard a testimony about a child who had a dream that he was giving his life to Jesus. It was so vivid that when he woke up that's just what he did!

> ### *I believe that as a body we need to prepare for the mass interpretation of dreams.*

Your nation is already dreaming but they don't know what their dreams mean. People will have destiny dreams, warning dreams, healing dreams, and training dreams, and we have to be ready as a Kingdom solution for them, ready to interpret by the Holy Spirit, whatever they throw at us!

You were a dream of God before you were born! Therefore, He gives you the dreams that He has already had about you. Expect dreams to alter your life just as happened with Joseph. Joseph had a dream, *but also the dream had him*. Never dismiss a dream with, "Oh, it's just a dream." After all, who knows what the angels had to fight through just to get that dream to you, just as in the days of Daniel! (See Daniel 10:12–14.)

It is time to raise your level of expectation for dreams.

PRAY

Jesus, I want to be sensitive to You in the night. Please submerge me in dream revelation from Your hand as I sleep.

I loose dreams all over this nation, that many will come to You through the invasion of Your Spirit in the night. In Jesus's name, amen!

A BLESSING

I pray for you, dear reader, and loose a godly avalanche of nighttime dreams and revelations to you, that you may know your Savior better as you sleep. In Jesus's name, amen!

7. Audible messages

One of the ways that God communicates with us is by His audible voice; we hear God speak aloud. Have you ever wondered what it must have been like at Jesus's baptism when *"a voice from heaven said, 'This is my Son, whom I love; with him I am well pleased'"*? (Matt. 3:17).

The Bible is full of examples of where people have heard God speak in an audible voice. For instance, Saul (and his traveling companions), as they were on the road to Damascus:

> [Saul] *fell to the ground and heard a voice say to him, "Saul, Saul, why do you persecute me?"*
>
> *"Who are you, Lord?" Saul asked.*
>
> *"I am Jesus, whom you are persecuting," he replied. "Now get up and go into the city, and you will be told what you must do."*
>
> *The men traveling with Saul stood there speechless; they heard the sound but did not see anyone* (Acts 9:4–7).

If you only *think* you have heard the audible voice of God then you probably haven't. You *know* when it is God! It is virtually indescribable.

Many years ago my parents pastored an international Baptist church in Spain. We were visiting them, and our family was sharing one large room. Everyone in the house was asleep except me, and I was outside on the balcony, warring with some demons who were on my parents' property. Returning into our room after dealing with that, I had a brief interaction with all my children's angels, who appeared to be on extra-high alert.

As I got back into bed, I was mulling over my favorite verse, from Psalm 46, a verse that I have often meditated through, over many years:

> *There is a river whose streams make glad the city of God, the holy place where the Most High dwells* (Psalm 46:4).

After a few minutes I drifted off to sleep.

Suddenly, I was physically shaken awake by God! His audible voice boomed loudly in the room and shook me to my core. He said to me, "*You* are a stream that makes Me glad."

With this there was no arguing, no questioning, no doubting, and no undermining.

It was so forceful, and yet so kind.

The voice arrested my insides and, in one short sentence, rewrote them.

8. Angelic visitations

It is biblically normal to interact with the angelic! Let's consider just how common it is.

- There are *seven* places in the New Testament where speaking in tongues is explicitly referred to.
- There is *one* place in scripture that describes putting out a fleece before God as Gideon did.
- There are over *three hundred* mentions of angels in Scripture. *One hundred and four* of these are interactions and visits with man.

It is more biblically common to interact with angels than it is to speak in tongues or to lay out our fleeces!

Angel or angels are mentioned *seventy-seven* times in Revelation, the final book of the Bible. This should suggest to us that we should expect a growing amount of angelic activity in the latter days. You should be seeing more angels and be aware of more angelic activity now than at any other point in history. The activity of angels will increase not decrease as the day of the Lord's return draws nearer.

Scripture considers many categories of angel, with different job descriptions. For example, Isaiah writes about *"the angel of his presence"* (Isa. 63:9); Psalm 91 describes what I call "hider angels," who are commanded to *guard* and *protect* us, keeping us under the shadow of their wings (see Ps. 91:1); there are Genesis 19 "destroyer angels" sent to destroy cities and deliver men (see Gen. 19:1, 13, 16); in First Kings 19 we read of angels who feed men (angels eating or preparing food seems to be quite a common theme in scripture); we know the choir of announcement angels at Bethlehem (see Luke 2:9–15); warrior angels in Daniel (see Dan. 10:13); and angels who look after the fiery coals of Heaven (see Isa. 6:1–7). And those are just for starters!

It is more biblically common to interact with angels than it is to speak in tongues.

Sometimes during a prophetic ministry session an angel will turn up with a message that we will have to relay to whoever is standing in front of us. Many times, my team will be aware of an angel entering the room with a new gift, mantle, or anointing. Working with the angels is very common for us at our center, especially in the intercession room. Angels hate to be worshipped and don't allow it. Never try to worship them; they will always send you to worship God instead, and if they don't, question who sent them. Neither should we command angels—only God does that. But we *are* to work with them as God sends them.

Perhaps Hebrews 1 provides the best definition of what angels in all their categories are sent to do: *"Are not all angels ministering spirits sent to serve those who will inherit salvation?"* (Heb. 1:14).

This means that there will be some angels whose specific job is an assignment to minster to you. The passage is past tense—the angels are *already* sent and active, it's just that you haven't been switched on to see them yet. Often at the end of busy and demanding days I can see and feel the angels laying hands on me and ministering to me while I sleep.

The angel of revelation

A huge part of how David and I got started in birthing Glasgow Prophetic Centre and the Global Prophetic Alliance network was through a friend's testimony of his interaction with an angel. His wild story awakened in me such a desire to know God and the fullness of His Kingdom that we set up training schools so that we could all hear and explore the *more* that God has for us.

My friend told us that he was sleeping one night when an angel physically shook him awake. The angel said that his assignment was as a revelation angel and he had things to say. At first my friend was skeptical, commenting that he wasn't sure that there was even a category of angels called "revelation angels." But when the angel indignantly replied, "I was on the Island of Patmos when John was given his revelation," my friend quietly backed down and let the angel instruct him. He took some notes on what the angel said and then went back to sleep.

Not long after, a demon shook my friend awake and snarled at him, "My name is Accusation!" From behind his back this demon brought out a large book and started to go through it, listing all the sins my friend had ever committed.

At that very moment, the angel of revelation reappeared. From behind his back he took the same book, but his was red and dripping in blood. The angel roared, "Here is the original copy; my master has dealt with it!" At this, the angel seemed to switch into fighting mode and drove the demon from the room, kicking and screaming.

My hider angel

One morning David left early to catch a red-eye flight to London for a day of meetings. I was alone in my bedroom when a regional strongman demon appeared at the end of my bed. I immediately got out of bed, turned my back on it, got onto my knees, and worshipped. He left, but intermittently reappeared throughout the day, eyeing me up, trying to intimidate. I asked God about it, and He told me, "It is the strongman of deception that oversees the lies that the people of Glasgow believe."

That night, David and I and another friend went out for dinner. We had just ordered food when the strongman demon reappeared. This time its arms were up in battle mode, and lots of smaller demons were rolling out of its cape and across the floor toward our table.

David saw my face and knew that I was seeing something. He asked if I needed to leave. "No way!" I replied, "I've just ordered my food."

I turned to my guardian angel for assistance, but he was already ten steps ahead of me. He turned his back on the demon, put his wings up and then arched them over and around us. He covered the three of us at the table (the angel was what I call a Psalm 91 "hider angel"[22]). From that moment on we became completely invisible to the rest of the restaurant. Seriously! None of the waitstaff noticed us. I actually had to go up to the kitchen hatch to retrieve our plates that had been ordered, prepared, and were now waiting for us!

By the end of the night we were the only ones left in the restaurant, all the other tables had been cleared and had upturned seats on them. As the staff were mopping the floor around our feet the demon gave up his futile intimidation and left. At this the angel put down his wings and suddenly the restaurant manager and all his staff were gathered around us. Question after question flowed from them: "How long have you been here? You are sitting at our most prominent table, how come none of us saw you all night? It was like you were invisible. How did you get your food? How come none of us saw you? How did you just appear right now in front of us when the restaurant door is locked? We'd already checked everywhere to see that everyone had left!" The manager was most apologetic for their lack of service and refused to charge us for our meal!

BE WILLING TO WORK WITH ANGELS

Like Paul in Corinthians, *"I do not know, but God knows"* (2 Cor. 12:2–3), there are some things that we cannot explain. Nevertheless, God expects a willingness in us to work with the angels that He sends us.

In Exodus 23:20–22 God says to Moses:

> *See, I am sending an angel ahead of you to guard you along the way and to bring you to the place I have prepared. Pay attention to him and listen to what he says. Do not rebel against him; he will not forgive your rebellion, since my Name is in him. If you listen carefully to what he says and do all that I say, I will be an enemy to your enemies and will oppose those who oppose you.*

God tells Moses that an angel is on the way. Moses is not only expected to see it, but he is also told to *pay attention* and *listen*. He is not just to open his eyes but also his ears, and he is told to obey the angel in a precise way. If he does this then God promises to be an enemy to Moses's enemies.

It's the same with Philip in Acts 8:26–27:

> *Now an angel of the Lord said to Philip, "Go south to the road–the desert road–that goes down from Jerusalem to Gaza." So he started out....*

All this should really alter our paradigm. We are so conditioned that we should only *look to see* the angels but then keep a safe distance, that we have lost the majority of the biblical truth of this. Which is that when angels turn up on God's business, we are to engage, dialogue, and be obedient.

Angels didn't become weakened at the end of the Bible. Neither did they decide that they would interact with us less. It is *we* who decided that this temporal world would be given a greater place in us than the spiritual world.

> **When angels turn up on God's business, we are to engage, dialogue, and be obedient.**

9. Trances

A trance is a stunned state, where a person's body is overwhelmed by the Spirit of God. The New Testament Greek word for trance is *ekstasis*, from which we get the word *ecstasy*. This world alone should suggest that they are a good thing! Often a person in a trance is stupefied, held, or arrested in some way and is goes into a *super-normal* state of mind. It is often a visional state, where revelation is received.

The word *trance* these days makes us nervous because it has been hijacked by the New Age and the occult. However, Scripture has many important examples of God-ordained, God-given trances. For example:

> *When I returned to Jerusalem and was praying at the temple, I fell into a trance* (Acts 22:17).

It is in this trance that Paul gets his instruction to take the gospel to the Gentiles. Had Paul not had this trance, it would have been a very different story for Christianity coming to the Gentiles—and that affects most of us reading this!

The entire history of the Church was changed by one experience of a trance. An entirely different way of interpreting Scripture was given. Gentiles came to faith in Jesus and Christianity was no longer viewed as being exclusively a Jewish faith.

Actually, the entire history of the Church was changed by *two* trance experiences! When Peter knocked on the door of Cornelius's household two days after his trance (Acts 10), he couldn't possibly have foreseen the billions of Gentiles, running to face their Redeemer, with Cornelius's household first in line.

Two Jewish men, two trances—the catalysts for the worldwide explosion of the gospel of the Kingdom!

The entire history of the church was changed by two trance experiences.

Falling into a trance whilst preaching

One day as I was preaching in a church in Glasgow God whispered in my ear. I was midsentence, but He said to me, "Lie down on the floor."

"But God I'm speaking!" I protested.

"Lie on the floor," He urged me again.

"God, look, I'm preaching. Are You sure?"

With a force He commanded, "Lie on the floor!"

I set down the microphone and lay down on the platform. To this day I'm still not entirely sure what happened to the hundreds of people who had been at the meeting, but when I came around an hour later, some of my team were on their knees, praying and worshipping near me.

Almost the very millisecond that I hit the floor, I fell into a deep trance. Jesus was with me, showing me different aspects of my sin. I was falling through time and space fast as lightning. As I fell down and down, I was seeing and realizing that parts of me were linked to demons in the darkness. Jesus never let go of me as I fell, repenting for all the ways my sin was interwoven in me. As I repented, ropes of captivity would fall off from me.

Once they were all gone, Jesus grabbed me and flew me upward and upward, toward His throne room. When we got there, He laid me down on the floor and started, with my permission, to pour a holy fire over me, burning me alive. Even in the trance it was agony, but it was a baptism of fire that has marked me for the years since.

Burning lips

That was not my first experience of being burnt by the fire of God. As a passionate eighteen-year-old I would run back from my lecture classes at university and fall onto my knees on my bedroom floor, reading Isaiah 6 and the description of how his lips were burned by the burning coals. For days I would get like this and beg God to do the same to me. One day a being, a *seraphim*, walked into the room with tongs and burned my lips. My mouth physically became ulcerated and bleeding inside (I still have the Bible that I bled over that day). In pain, I went to my minister for help. He poured me a glass of water, blessed it, and I drank it. My mouth healed as quickly as it had begun to bleed.

God wants us to be a flame of fire, a fire-baptized son or daughter.

> *I have come to bring fire on the earth, and how I wish it were already kindled!* (Luke 12:49)

Trances are God-led

Trances are God-led and God-inspired. I will not (nor should anyone else) teach you *how* to achieve them.

> *But our God is in the heavens; He does whatever He pleases* (Psalm 115:3 NASB).

Rather, I want you to know that trances are real, and they are biblical. You should not reject a trance if God chooses to take you into His revelatory ocean through the door of one.

10. Out-of-body experiences and translations

An out-of-body experience, or "translation," is where your body stays in one place, but your spirit travels to another. The Christian form of this is *always* God-driven and God-led.

Again, as with trances, I cannot teach you how to do this. You must wait on the Lord to experience this. New Agers have their own evil version called astral projection. They differ from us because they induce this at their own will.

Ezekiel is the prime biblical example of a person who had out-of-body experiences. He cites at least six times where this happens to him. Ezekiel tends to describe it in the words, *"then the Spirit lifted me up."*

Paul also talks about this kind of experience, where he was *caught up* to the third Heaven:

> *I know a man in Christ who fourteen years ago was caught up to the third heaven. Whether it was in the body or out of the body I do not know–God knows. And I know that this man–whether in the body or apart from the body I do not know, but God knows– was caught up to paradise and heard inexpressible things, things that no one is permitted to tell* (2 Corinthians 12:2–4).

Similarly, John in Revelation:

> *After this I looked, and there before me was a door standing open in heaven. And the voice I had first heard speaking to me like a trumpet said, "Come up here, and I will show you what must take place after this." At once I was in the Spirit...* (Revelation 4:1–2).

We must not let the enemy steal what God has ordained. We must choose to not be afraid of the unusual ways of the Holy Spirit.

This experience is common for me and many of my family and team. We are quite used to God *catching us up* and showing us amazing things! I often ask God how He is feeling or what is He is up to today. He loves to show us!

Restroom encounter

In the middle of a challenging ministry trip God caught me up in the spirit. It was moments before I was due to speak, and I had just nipped out of the front row to the use the restroom! Whilst in the restroom, God said, "Come up here! You need to see something immediately before you preach another word here!"

The poison arrow tip

Perhaps one of the most unusual encounters I've ever had was one night in London. It all started with a dream in my sleep, but halfway through something changed and I was no longer aware whether I was *in the spirit* or actually somewhere else, whether God had physically moved me to another location.

I was chasing demons with a team, and we were deep underground. The demonic hordes were on the retreat; I could see battalions of demons retreating from the earth for a while. But in the midst of this, from somewhere, a poison arrow tip was pushed into my arm. I fell to the ground and thought, "Oh, this must be what it is like to die." I could feel the breath leaving my body.

> ## We must choose to not be afraid of the unusual ways of the Holy Spirit.

Suddenly, I am back in London and wide awake (not waking up) and standing (not lying down) in the middle of the room. I ran to the bathroom and managed to start breathing again. I switched on the light and looked down at my arm. There in my arm was a real, physical, arrow-tipped puncture mark. For days later poison dripped out of the wound.

Some great advisors helped me navigate the interpretation of this experience and why God had given permission for it to happen. It was real in ways that I don't truly understand. We are touching the mystery of God and working with Him, according to His agenda and not our own.

TOP TIP

In prayer times when you feel like God wants to take you some-where or show you something, be brave and don't resist God. Linger when you are in a "thin place."

For me, I can feel Him pulling me backward, pulling me out of this world and into His.

11. Transportations

Supernatural transportation or "translocation" is more properly defined as an actual physical experience, not just a vision. It is where God takes you physically from one location and puts you in another. For example, in Acts 8 we read that Philip is physically moved:

> *When they came up out of the water, the Spirit of the Lord sud-denly took Philip away, and the eunuch did not see him again, but went on his way rejoicing* (Acts 8:39).

Elijah receives a version of this after Mount Carmel:

*The power of the L<small>ORD</small> came upon Elijah and, tucking his
cloak into his belt, he ran ahead of Ahab all the way to Jezreel*
(1 Kings 18:46).

Elijah is transported by the power of the Lord beyond what is
physically, humanly possible.

And Jesus Christ "transports" on *at least* two occasions:

*Then their eyes were opened and they recognized him, and he
disappeared from their sight* (Luke 24:31).

*While they were still talking about this, Jesus himself stood
among them and said to them, "Peace be with you"* (Luke
24:36).

12. Third Heaven encounters

You can visit "third Heaven," be "caught up to Heaven" in a
variety of ways that I've already described: either in an open or
closed vision, an out-of-body experience, where your spirit is taken
up, or in a transportation, where you *physically* go. Most often in my
life God shows me Heaven in a vision or an out-of-body experience.

Ezekiel saw Heaven, as did Isaiah, John, Paul, Jacob, and Daniel.
There are living creatures and a sea of glass, there is thunder and
lightning, and God has seated you there beside Jesus, who is at His
right hand. He wants you to meet with Him there. As a believer who
is seated in heavenly places, you can ascend and descend and enter
in; it's the place that Jesus's blood gave you access to.

When my daughter was first taken to the throne room by Jesus,
she was still very young. On her "return" she described the living
creatures perfectly, even though she had never at that point read
about them in Scripture.

He is the God of miracles.

ENCOUNTERS WITH JESUS

It's quite a list that we have just gone through in this chapter! Although we use all these types of encounters to bring prophecy or revelation to others, the overriding reason for all of them is that *we get to encounter Jesus.*

> ### *It's the place that Jesus's blood gave you access to.*

In all of the supernatural encounters that I have had, they have driven me to a new level of holy "miserableness," where I have seen His glory and love Him, and yet I am even more aware of my own sin in light of His holiness. I say I love Him with all my heart, but sometimes these encounters make me see how painfully disconnected I really am.

Encounters drive us to worship, drive us to our knees, and give us responsibility to steward what has been shown.

> ### *Can God be Himself with you, or do you only want **your** version of Him?*

Most of us have been raised to think in an over-logical way. We rightly enjoy our ability to analyze, but it has gone too far into a state of overanalysis, so much so that we see cynicism as the sign of maturity.

Everything that I have shared with you in this chapter is contrary to the wisdom of man. We have touched areas that seem so far-fetched to our Western mindset. These experiences touch areas of sovereignty and mystery that we will simply never understand.

God, more than anything, is looking for friends. He only calls a very select few His friends in Scripture. I believe that, sadly, God turns up in churches and often stays in the hallway, because the people will not let Him come in as He is. They want *their* version of Him. God cannot therefore be Himself with them. Friends are themselves with each other. Can God be Himself with you, or do you only want *your* version of Him?

So how are you doing with the list of how God speaks and encounters His revelatory people? If you would like to meet with God in all the ways that He outlines in Scripture, it's time to pray.

PRAY

Father, I am undone that You want to draw me into revelatory encounters. I say yes to You, and I give You the space to be who You are.

I am sorry for the times that I have shut down encounters and was cynical about the extremes of Your Kingdom and its ways. Please take me by the hand and lead me into deeper places. I want to go on a new adventure with You.

In Jesus's name, amen!

CHAPTER 11

The Sound of Good Prophecy

Excellence is the unlimited ability to improve the quality of what you have to offer.

—Rick Pitino, Basketball Coach

As we have journeyed through faith, war, and prophecy, we have understood the importance of hearing from God. But I believe that merely settling for this in and of itself is not enough for a prophetic warrior. A prophetic warrior must coura-geously, and with great determination, pursue *excellence* in the gift.

In this final chapter we will look at what makes "good" prophecy and what parameters and frameworks must be understood in order to bring forth credibility and excellence. We will be considering questions like, "What are the biblical building blocks that the gift of prophecy must stand upon?"

GOOD PROPHECY: SOUNDS LIKE FINDING THE GOLD

Some of you reading this will have received prophetic words that left you feeling disappointed, discouraged, rebuked, and even verbally slapped across the face. Many people have told to me that they are scared of prophecy, fearing that someone with a prophetic gift will expose all their sins.

The tongue has the power of life and death (Proverbs 18:21).

You can speak and create utter havoc, or you can bring break-through and life by what you say. What you say has creative power. Words leave you and they go to accomplish and establish. Words do not hang in the atmosphere, loitering and wondering if they should have impact. Words always have impact!

Our responsibility as prophetic people is that we must guard our tongues. There must be a greater watch over what we say.

At some point someone will stand in front of you to receive a pro-phetic word. You know the power of the tongue and you know the scripture that if you *"decree a thing, and it will be established"* (Job 22:28 NASB). What do think will happen if you speak with judgment, anger, criticism, and unkindness, perhaps seeking to point-score or push your own agenda? You will create fear, intimidation, anx-iety, and shame, and you will belittle the recipient. Speaking with meanness and retribution does damage. It must *never* become our prophetic model.

Prophecy is a privilege, and we come to it respecting the biblical code:

> *But the one who prophesies speaks to people for their strengthen-ing, encouraging and comfort* (1 Corinthians 14:3).
> *But one who prophesies speaks to men for edification and exhor-tation and consolation* (1 Corinthians 14:3 NASB).

Strengthening, encouragement, comfort, edification, exhortation, and consolation—that's quite a list! There are no exclusions to this. You cannot tamper with this biblical principle. This means that these kinds of comments are *not* allowed: "I see such darkness in you," "Look at that sin," or "I just feel like God is asking me to point out where you have gone wrong."

> **What you say has creative power. Words leave you and they go to accomplish and establish.**

Perhaps the worst that I've heard was someone telling a lady in a practice session that we were facilitating that she was "like that prostitute in Scripture who Hosea married"! And this was despite me explaining that this kind of thing was not allowed!

We all want the Church to be able to receive those with a prophetic gift, but if you only use your platform to "put people right," church leaders would be wise to remain suspicious of those who carry revelation.

No criticism or judgment must creep in. We must not do the Holy Spirit's job for Him. Only He convicts of sin. We are not in trainee Holy Spirit positions.

Prophecy activates godly motivation; it triggers people to make decisions for the better. It becomes the horizon line for someone's life; it becomes where they aim. If you can help them to see the future that God wants for them, it will reshape their life. How far one can see, is how one will plan today for one's destiny. The more you see, the more you will expect.

THE PROPHETIC WARRIOR

People are usually already well aware of their own issues and sin. They don't need you to remind them. What they have forgotten, however, is the call of God and the dreams and the treasures that He has stored inside them. It takes a very low-grade person and a low-grade prophetic gift to point out sin.

Revelation is powerful. It changes you immediately. Prophecy brings shape to what is sagging, gives purpose to what is wayward, and gives life to that which is dying. Prophecy legislates for the Kingdom of God and cancels out the whispering voice of the enemy.

Prophecy activates godly motivation; it triggers people to make decisions for the better. It becomes the horizon line for someone's life; it becomes where they aim.

WHAT ABOUT WHEN YOU SEE THE NEGATIVE?

Of course, you *will* see the negative; you *will* see and sense people's pain and issues. What do you do then?

For example, we often see depression on people. But there are many ways that you can share that revelation.

1. *With irritation—angry and judgmentally*: for example, saying "I see depression on you" with a facial expression that communicates, "What a failure you are!" But the person already knew that they had it.

All you have done is just magnified the problem. (So, don't do this!)

2. *Gravely and without victory:* for example, saying, "I see depression on you" with a tone of voice that conveys that there is no hope for the person. (Don't do this either!)

3. *Prophetically, biblically knowing you can sow either death or life.* Go back to God and ask, "God, what's the solution to this depression that I see?" For example, it might sound like this: "God is sending a wave of healing joy to wash over you. You will find yourself in your right mind and with a new strategy for your future. God is sending laughter to your home and a gladness to your heart. He is removing the weights from the previous season and a freedom is coming to you now!"

Did you notice that there was no mention of depression? This way you have not exposed their pain, but *they* will know that you have seen it and will be grateful that you brought the healing, rescuing word of God.

I challenge you: How much life can you prophetically bring to others?

FIND THE GOLD
AND ARCHITECTING HOPE

Therefore, thus says the Lord, *"If you return, then I will restore you—before Me you will stand; and if you extract the precious from the worthless, you will become My spokesman"* (Jeremiah 15:19 NASB).

We need to speak that which brings into focus the treasures, the precious, the gold. God's prophetic people can extract the precious from the worthless and can bring breakthrough when things seems impenetrable.

Our in-house phrase that we say back and forth to each other is "find the gold"!

All mankind is made in the image of God, and He wants that none of us would perish—after all, it is His loving-kindness that brings us to repentance (see Rom. 2:4). You can find gold even in the midst of a lost person's sinful fallenness, where they need a radical, repentant lifestyle turnaround. Despite our own prejudices you can still find gold in homosexuals, heterosexuals, thieves, liars, murderers, adulterers, pedophiles, males, females, transgenders, socialists, capitalists, fascists, communists, Muslims, Hindus, Baptists, atheists, Anglicans, politicians, Scots, English, Africans, and Americans! At our center we have prophesied over people from every single one of these categories, and more!

If you feel full of pain, if you are full of anger and bitterness, or if you are irritated with people, you will not prophesy well. In fact, *you should not prophesy at all.*

> *God's prophetic people can extract the precious from the worthless and can bring breakthrough when things seems impenetrable.*

This truth does not mean that all we can bring are sweet words about flowers, fluffy clouds, cotton candy, or pretty sailing boats!

When we are told in First Corinthians 14:3 *"strengthening, encouraging and comfort"* what do these three words really mean?

Strengthening

This means (the act of) building; building up; spiritual advancement; constructive criticism and instruction that builds a person up to be the suitable dwelling place of God (in other words, where the Lord is "at home"). You are architecting hope. You are bringing constructive words without vile criticism. There is a vigor to this concept; it is not mealymouthed.

Encouraging

This is translated from the Greek word *paraclete*, which is a legal term for evidence that stands up in a court. (This is also the word used in John for the Holy Spirit, meaning you have an on-board lawyer living inside you!) It means to urge and appeal, to deliver God's verdict. In other words, prophecies that reveal how the Lord weighs the relevant facts. It is used to describe God directly motivating and inspiring believers to carry out His plan. Again, as with strengthening, there is a loving determination to this: bringing words that urge and propel a person forward to walk out the plans of God.

Comfort

This of course means to speak with tenderness, having the personal touch.

God expects us to be able to deliver a tender, personal word that builds hope, urges people forward, and delivers the verdict of God in any situation.

The witch who came to curse

One time, a witch from a local coven emailed us to say she was planning to come to a public event where we were prophesying. She warned us that she was going to curse us. At this, I thought to myself, *"Ha! All the best with that; we are not deserving of curses so your words will have no effect!"* (See Proverbs 26:2.)

> **Deliver a tender, personal word that builds hope, urges people forward, and delivers the verdict of God in any situation.**

She turned up at the event, spoke in a demonic, snakelike tongue, trying to intimidate everyone. I told her that I had a word for her and was going to prophesy over her. I duly escorted her to a seat; all the while she never let up with her cursing chant.

I prayed: "What do You want me to say God?"

He told me, "Tell her that My blood was shed as much for her as it was for you and that you are sorry that Christians were so unkind to her in her childhood years." I passed on the message to her.

At this, she began to weep. By now she clearly didn't know whether she should be cursing or sobbing, so she tried to do both at once! The word of the Lord to her continued: "God wants to know why you are looking for the living amongst the dead? He says that you have a tarot card reading booked for this week, and when you go, in that place you will have a revelation that Jesus is the way, the truth, and the life. When this happens, turn up at this address [I gave her an address]."

She left the event undone, expectant, challenged, and loved, despite all her previous best efforts to be difficult, rude, and to curse.

Jesus did in fact reveal Himself to her few days later, in the heart of the medium's room where she was having a reading. She went to the address that I had given her, and the people there prayed for healing for a long-term back problem that she had been carrying. She was saved, healed, and delivered by the end of the week. Praise God!

GOOD PROPHECY: SOUNDS LIKE A FLOW

The phrase "to prophesy" in Hebrew Scripture is *naba*. The prophets were called *nabi*, but they *naba* what they heard from God. *Naba* means to bubble up, to pour forth, to flow and to have an abundance of words. And you can either speak the words or sing them out.

Abraham, Iddo, Zechariah, Asaph, Gad, Amos, Heman, Habakkuk, Jeduthan, Samuel, Isaiah, Jeremiah, Ezekiel, Daniel, Joel, Obadiah, Jonah, Micah, and Malachi (to name but a few!) all had a *naba* flow; we find the word *naba* in the biblical texts associated with these prophets.

Now, despite its meaning, *naba* is not the ability to say a lot of words for word's sake, with sentences that go on and on and on and on and on—like a raving extrovert who cannot be stopped! Rather, *naba* is the ability to flow in the words of prophecy that land right at the core of a situation, and like a well-fitting key, unlock and bring life.

Prophetic checkups

Years ago, I got very frustrated with receiving prophetic words that were under three minutes long and only scratched the surface of life. Because my background before full-time ministry was in phar-maceuticals and I was used to "medical checkups," the concept of having a "prophetic checkup" appointment was born. We have now been offering forty-five-minute-long checkups at Glasgow Prophetic Centre for the last eleven years, with the team having generated at minimum an estimated *thirty-five thousand hours of personal prophetic ministry*! Each team member (we minister in teams of three or four) trains in a *nabi* flow so that they can prophesy at length, going deep with the Holy Spirit and deep into a person's life, so that their words can bring godly order, healing, and forward movement.

The Holy Spirit carries seeds

When you *naba* it is not just your breath that the words are car-ried on. The Holy Spirit also carries the words and then *lands them*. You *must* partner with the Holy Spirit for a *naba* flow. Prophecy necessitates a reliance on the Holy Spirit, a love of Him, and a rela-tionship with Him. The Holy Spirit enables a *naba* abundance of words to flow out of you, as He bubbles up from the inside of you.

> **Naba** *is the ability to flow in the words of prophecy that land right at the core of a situation, and like a well-fitting key, unlock and bring life.*

The Bible often uses the metaphor of a seed to describe God's Word.[23] I like to think of *naba* being the process of putting a word inside of someone, like a farmer planting a seed. That is why it is so important that what we say is carried on the Spirit. The Holy Spirit carries the word and plants it right into the spirit of the person that you are speaking to. Then, when it is planted in the right place, it can grow and change a life!

Some folks can look really off-putting when you prophesy over them—their body language is slumped, they look like they are chewing a wasp, they give off that they are full of depression and sullenness. It is easy to therefore make the assumption, "I must prophesy about joy!" and then get the word all wrong. *Never* prophesy to the physical presentation of a person.

TOP TIP

When prophesying, try to avoid commenting on what a person is wearing. Don't mention that you feel drawn to their scarf, necklace, or jewelry. This just opens the door to people-reading rather than following the Holy Spirit.

Spirit to spirit

When you *naba*, you go past a person's skin and presentation and you prophesy spirit to spirit. We want to be people who prophesy spirit to spirit and not flesh to flesh. It's never a word for their ego.

The reason that we read that none of Samuel's words fell to the ground[24]—they didn't spill out of him and just land on the floor at his feet—is because they were carried by a *naba* Holy Spirit flow, and they flew right to where they would have an impact!

Naba words land and are hard to shake off. They resonate and rattle in you, remaining for years as hope for the future.

When you are planting a seed, people occasionally get angry or weep. Why? They have forgotten who God made them to be. You sow, the seed grows, and it is different from how they are right now, and this rattles them. Often the demonic comes out as we prophesy a seed in; the seed can displace the demon, and it is perfectly normal on occasions to have some demonic manifestation as you sow into a person's life. In fact, the force of a seed landing can shock *everyone* in the room, as the Holy Spirit plants something that will not be lost. That seed will remain in them all their days.

PRAYER

Jesus, I want to prophesy with a flow of Your words, not with fits and starts but with an unfolding revelation. Jesus, would You release me into a naba flow, where I sow seeds of truth and life.

In Jesus's name, amen!

GOOD PROPHECY: USES ALL THE REVELATORY TOOLS

First Corinthians lists nine spiritual gifts that the Holy Spirit gives (1 Cor. 12:7–11). Of these, five are revelatory in nature. It is important to know what they all do and how we might best apply them. The five revelatory gifts of the Spirit are:

1. Prophecy
2. Word of Wisdom
3. Word of Knowledge
4. Discerning of Spirits
5. Interpretation of Tongues

Good prophecy weaves all these revelatory tools together. Let's consider each one.

Prophecy

Prophecy is being a spokesperson for God. It is where you speak whatever message God wants said. You declare the mind of God. You represent God however He wants to be seen, however He wants to sound, and whatever He wants to say. Sometimes this is about the future. Future prediction is something that some prophets do sometimes, but it is not the main biblical role of someone who prophesies. Future prediction is calling the uncreated future to form and come into being. It is not fortune-telling but is instead seeing the future as God intends it to be. Often this means pointing forward to the highest and best for a person, nation, or situation.

I believe that our main role in prophecy is to be malleable and flexible enough that you speak what God wants and not what you want. You become a herald, speaking as an official messenger for God.

In prophecy you declare the mind of God. You represent God however He wants to be seen, however He wants to sound, and whatever He wants to say.

Word of wisdom

A word of wisdom knows what *action* needs taken. It is different from the wisdom that Solomon asks for, which is a general wisdom and a skill for living. The revelatory gift of a word of wisdom gives an often-unusual strategy for what action must be taken to see change come.

Once, when sitting with clients who had marriage intimacy issues, God said, "If they will buy different colored bed sheets, there will be a renewed ease in the marriage bed." This certainly sounded a bit strange to us all; surely that's never how these painful things heal. However, it was God's bespoke strategy in this situation. They bought the bed linen, and God healed their issues in an instant!

When Noah was told to build an ark, it was a specific, unique word of wisdom from God, an action required in a moment of time. Asking God, "What must this person do?" will lead you to a word of wisdom.

A word of wisdom gives a strategy for what action must be taken to see change come.

Word of knowledge

A word of knowledge is a fact that can be measured as either right or wrong and is given to unlock a person to further words from God. Such facts display the nature of God who knows that person intimately.

Jesus uses a word of knowledge with the Samaritan women at the well (see John 4:18). By Jesus's telling her that she had had five husbands, the woman knew that she was known, and it totally undoes her, leading to an awakening across her town.

My daughter Jessica asked me recently if she could come traveling with me when I ministered. I explained that she could take a seat on a plane just as soon as she could happily take a microphone and prophecy the moment we landed in a new destination. At the time she was fifteen and desperate to have adventure.

So, she went out with her friends into the city, determined to find someone to prophesy over in order to prove that she was ready. She walked up to the most demonized-looking lady on the street and told her that she was a Christian and that God had given her a word for her. The lady rudely said that she was a witch and that there was nothing that Jessica could say that would turn her affections (and some other choice words).

But Jessica had a word of knowledge for her and, before the she could walk away, countered, "God has told me you have just been diagnosed with breast cancer and that if you put your hand on the lump, as a sign that God loves you He will heal it and it will disappear." Without further protest, the lady reached up and put her hand across the breast lump. God healed it on the spot, and it disappeared!

The word of knowledge is very powerful in prophetic evangelism as you are able to open a door to someone's life and heart by releasing facts about them. This can often look quite spectacular, but remember that *we are to be comfortable with the supernatural rather than fixated with the spectacular*. Always build a word of prophecy on top of the word of knowledge, so that the person might move beyond being impressed only and into meeting God fully.

ACTIVATION

This gift takes bravery because the recipient will tell you right there and then if you are right or wrong. Ask God to tell you where someone has pain or sickness in their body. Be brave and tell them what you have seen and then heal them.

Discerning of spirits

The word *discern* means to distinguish between. In other words, it's about knowing the difference between spirits. This is important to be able to do because the word *spirit* can mean lots of things, including angels, demons, the human spirit, the Holy Spirit, anointing, mantles, or the motivating influence of a person.

> *We are to be comfortable with the supernatural rather than fixated with the spectacular.*

This gift is therefore the supernatural ability to discern spirits right across the spectrum. It is this gift that will keep you safe. It will give you the ability to navigate the spirit realm without harm.

Discerning of spirits is an underused and overlooked gift that is your greatest weapon to enjoying the spirit realm.

> *Discerning of spirits is an underused and overlooked gift that is your greatest weapon to enjoying the spirit realm.*

There are three main sources of spirit to be discerned:

1. human spirits

2. Holy Spirit(s)

3. demonic spirits

Let's briefly consider each of these areas.

Human spirits

It is fundamental in life that we can monitor the state of our own spirit. We don't do this in an introspective way but instead so that we can line up with how God intended the inside of us to be. We must not be easily tossed about *emotionally.*

King David had a great handle on discerning the human spirit:

> *Why, my soul, are you downcast? Why so disturbed within me?* (Psalm 42:5)

David looks at his own spirit, sees what is going on and then gives it some good medicine:

> *Put your hope in God, for I will yet praise him, my Savior and my God* (Psalm 42:5).

In the next verse he seems to retest his spirit and finds that again, "*My soul is downcast within me.*" And so, he medicates it again by saying:

> *...therefore I will remember you from the land of the Jordan, the heights of Hermon–from Mount Mizar* (Psalm 42:6).

In this Psalm David discerns his spirit and then actions what he sees.

We also read of David "[strengthening] *himself in the* Lord *his God*" in First Samuel 30:6 (NKJV). In the preceding verses, David has just returned to his camp at Ziklag to find that his wives have been captured by the Amalekites. We read that he wept until he had no strength left. Afterward, David is further distressed because his men are plotting to stone him because all their wives and children have been taken as well.

In this moment, David's human spirit is ravished with grief and pain; the inside of him is churned in knots. And yet he does not let it overwhelm him and he *"finds strength in the LORD."* The prophet Larry Randolph says that, "God is not responsible for making us reach our own potential."[25] The call of God on *your* life requires *your* participation. It requires *you* to be self-aware and to manage the inside of *you*.

God brings moments into our lives when we must stand alone in difficulty and testing. God will even blind the eyes and deafen the ears of our closest friends in those moments so that we can learn how to minister to ourselves and strengthen ourselves in the Lord. We must recognize this or else we will fall into bitterness and rejection from thinking that our friends have let us down in these hard times.

So how do you strengthen yourself in the Lord? What is it you do when your human spirit and emotions are overwhelmed or not lining up with the Word of God? When you look inside and you see that your human spirit is fearful, angry, broken, a bit down, not at peace, what are the top ways you strengthen yourself and get your human spirit back on track? Here's one: self-talk.

If we are honest with ourselves, have we have allowed the melancholy and inaccuracy of internal self-talk to get the better of us? Have we subsequently had days when we have spiraled down outside of God's best?

Your internal dialogue is about fifteen hundred words per minute. This goes up when you have had caffeine. So, the average person is probably *wrestling with three to four ungodly beliefs every minute*. Is it any wonder that we must strengthen ourselves in the Lord!

Some of us have listened to the enemy's voices for so long that we can't discern which is ours and which is satan's. God wants to heal you of destructive, boundaryless, internal dialogues.

As a rule, anything that is condemning is not from God. His correction is different from condemnation. Condemnation is either the enemy or your partnership with what the enemy sent. Unrighteous, unpeaceful, unjoyful, and fear-based thoughts are *not* from God.

The most important relationship that you have, apart from the one you have with God, is the one that you have with yourself. How *you* feel about *you* will affect everything else, and if you can't reach in and strengthen yourself, you will be overwhelmed. Prophetic warriors, you lost the right to beat yourself up when you got saved!

> **Anything that is condemning is not from God.**

ACTIVATION

Meditate on these questions:

- When I discern that my human spirit is out of line, what is my personal weapon against this?
- How do I strengthen myself in the Lord?

- What is it that makes me regroup?
- What is the thing that I do when I am feeling low that shifts me back to who God says I am?

Holy Spirit

We are continuing to look at the three kinds of spirit that we can distinguish between. In the category of Holy Spirit, we also set angelic spirits, sent by God.

We want to keep a pace with what the Holy Spirit is doing. The gift of discerning of spirits will reveal the direction and flow that the Holy Spirit is going in.

I remember asking the Holy Spirit before a freedom ministry session to tell me how many demons He wanted us to deal with in the next client's life. The Holy Spirit answered, "Three." The client came in for his appointment, and two hours later we had chased down *sixteen* different supposed demons before it finally dawned on us that we were dealing with a lying spirit! A salutary tale that I should have followed the Holy Spirit with greater diligence.

Have you ever heard someone say, "God is telling me take an action," and you think to yourself, "I don't think He really is at all!"

Have you ever taken a decision that you were *sure* was God, only to later reflect that it probably wasn't God at all?

One of the key questions in life is to know exactly what the Holy Spirit is currently doing. This gift will take you from being unsure what the Holy Spirit is saying into hearing with total clarity.

In addition, the discerning of spirits gift is like a door or a gate. Once you have it, it opens up a whole new realm. You go from *not knowing* what is in the sprit realm, to *knowing* what's there. The discerning of spirits is the gift of access to the spirit realm. It is not just about assessing or judging what's happening in a detached way; it's also the ability to *partake* in the spirit realm.

Also, just to be clear, it is *not* a people-reading gift; it is a *spirit-reading* gift.

> **One of the key questions in life is to know exactly what the Holy Spirit is currently doing.**

ACTIVATION

In this activation there are some questions to help you with looking into the supernatural, (holy) spiritual realm. These questions are not a formula (we don't do magic formulas!); they are simply a basic tool to get you activated in seeing.

1. Ask God to show you a spiritual door in the room you are in.
2. Look through the door, to the other side. If the door is closed, you may have to open it to see through. Where does it go to?
3. Ask God to show you why the door is there. What's the purpose of the door?
4. Go through the door and enjoy what God shows you on the other side of it.

Demonic spirits

This aspect of the gift of discerning of spirits will reveal specific demonic spirits that are hindering, shadowing, or demonizing you or another person. It can be helpful to partner this with a word of knowledge in order to reveal the circumstances and time *when* the demonic spirit entered. But the discerning of spirits will reveal *what type* of spirit is present.

At times it can be challenging to accurately assess what demonic shadows are swirling around our own lives. In my own life God lets me stand in front of a heavenly mirror and then I can see, in the reflection, what is prowling around me and what needs dealt with.

The gift will also reveal demonic principalities and powers over a geographical area. For example, in Scotland we have demonic territorial spirits of religion and of freemasonry.

We do *not* focus on the demons that we see. We simply acknowledge that they are there and that they need to be removed. If I focus on demons and what they put in front of me, that focus will become part of who I am. If I focus on Jesus, then I become more like Him. Always focus on Jesus!

If you have ever felt like a city without walls, easily overwhelmed and often unprotected and defenseless, then you need to ask for this gift so that you might see and discern what is happening around you in the spirit realm. This gift will strengthen your ability to stand in any atmosphere that you walk into.

PRAYER

Jesus, I repent that I have not discerned spirits and
that they have tossed me to-and-fro. I am sorry.

Jesus, I invite You to give me courage to stand. I repent for any ways that I have come under demonic spirits—or my own spirit—instead of releasing Your Kingdom.

Jesus, I ask that You would release to me the fullness of the gift of the discerning of Spirits. I receive it now.

In Your name I pray, amen!

This gift will strengthen your ability to stand in any atmosphere that you walk into.

Interpretation of tongues

The fifth revelatory gift is the ability to understand, in your own language, what is being said in the language of Heaven. This gift is one of the gifts that is most missing from the day-to-day life of the Spirit-filled Church today. And yet, when it is used well, there is great power and breakthrough!

This gift requires courageous teamwork: one to bring the word in tongues and another to interpret the word. As with the other gifts, you really need to practice, practice, practice!

If you are weak in any of these five revelatory areas, ask God to develop them in you and then start practicing with your friends!

GOOD PROPHECY: HAS A SHAPE

Past, present, and future

In good prophetic words there tends to be an *arc of revelation* that begins in the past by unveiling previous life events. This is then followed by a moment of clarity on the present that gives context for what is happening today. Finally, there is a forthtelling concerning the future that brings hope. Past, present, and future: all key elements of a good word.

The revelation of the past will bring healing and will enable a greater weight of expectation to be opened about the future. In prophesying this, you are proving that God knows the past and therefore that He can also be trusted to know what is ahead.

However, one of the major Achilles heels of the prophetic movement is to get stuck in the past and so turn a prophetic word into a counselling or shepherding session. This is a continual battle that prophetic people must wrestle with, that they take off the glasses of the shepherds (who naturally want to focus on lifelong nurture) and they put on the glasses of the prophetic that seeks to release a sharpening and clarity of where destiny lies.

Remembering that you are bringing revelation on the present and future, as well as the past, will help you to avoid this trap.

Revelation, interpretation, and application

The second arc that we must be mindful of is revelation, interpretation, and application. A prophetic word will start with a *revelation* as a picture, or sense, or word. It is then your job to bring an *interpretation* that expands what the revelation means and then the *application* of how it is to be applied or worked with. We must learn to hold revelation until it is mature and we have the best clarity possible at our disposal. Maturity does not interrupt and seek attention; it does not rush forward during church services and demand to be heard!

> **Remember that you are bringing revelation on the present and future, as well as the past.**

On Sunday mornings, when the preacher has spent at least fifteen hours in prayer and preparation to preach and teach a message, and you get an unresolved prophetic "something" in five minutes during worship and then become demanding to share it. Well, don't be surprised if you're asked to take your seat. It's not that the revelation might be wrong, it's often simply the case that interpretation and application are lacking. Most words can wait a few days.

One trainee who worked with me in a session brought a word about cows to a client. She "prophesied" that "the cows are in the field, the cows are in the barn, the cows are walking down the farm road, the cows are at the farmhouse—there are cows everywhere and I have no idea what this means so I will just leave it with you."

> **We must learn to hold revelation until it is mature and we have the best clarity possible at our disposal.**

Don't bring unresolved words! Ask God what the word or picture means and what the recipients are to do with it.

Perhaps the strangest application or ending to a prophetic word that I ever heard from God was at an outdoor Christian festival.

Days before we had traveled to the event, one of my team had prophesied over me that I would stand in front of hermaphrodites and people who had had sex-change operations, their bodies would be called back to order and that body parts would grow (and other parts would drop off).

Well, at the end of my time speaking at the festival I was ministering to a line of people in turn, when I heard myself say over one woman, "I call your womb to grow in Jesus's name!"

Stopping to chat, she told me that she had been born with no functioning sexual organs. The woman was married and desperate for children. Praying for her, I then listed all the female reproductive organs, calling them to form in Jesus's name. She was doubled over as Jesus worked on her insides.

The word needed testing; we had to have an application. I gave her my compact makeup mirror and sent her to the mobile restroom units in the field outside. Soon after she came running back, declaring that there was an opening in her body that only women have that wasn't there before we had prayed! God had worked a creative miracle and had given her new and functioning sexual organs!

Telling people that you see a picture from God and that you'll leave it with them is *poor prophecy*. Working with God to hear the interpretation and application, asking questions like, "*What do You mean by this God?*" and "*What should they do next?*" will help you prophesy well.

GOOD PROPHECY:
CONTAINS BIBLICAL ILLUSTRATIONS

The best prophetic voices reference scripture all through their words. I am always worried when prophecies only say, "Did you see such and such film? God is speaking to you through it" or "Did you see this TV program? Because what happened in it is happening in your life." We might, at times, successfully use these cultural references but our revelation must also have biblical anecdotes, quotes, and stories peppered through it. This will perpetually keep us anchored in truth.

This necessitates that our lives meditate on the Word of God. When the Word of God dwells richly in you, it will increase your Holy Spirit vocabulary. Good and trusted prophetic warriors know their Bibles inside and out and are voracious readers of the Word of God.

Give yourself to the reading of the Word; know God through it and how He does and does not communicate. We must get past the immature idea that "a verse a day keeps the devil at bay" by reading Scripture in large chunks, as it was intended by the original writers. Many years ago my father stopped calling his time with God his "quiet time" and now calls it his "joy time." Maybe you too need to change how you think and approach your time with God and His Word.

Good and trusted prophetic warriors know their Bibles inside and out.

263

PRAY

God, would You give me a passion for Your Word, an insatiable appetite for Your truth, that I might live a life washed in it and infused by it.

In Jesus's name, amen!

MY PRAYER FOR YOU

I pray for you that all sleepiness and distraction when you read the Bible would be broken off you right now and that focus and energy would accompany your Bible reading.

I loose to you the ability to memorize scripture with ease!

In Jesus's name, amen!

TOP TIP

The more you speak in tongues throughout your day, the more you have the words of Heaven already in your mouth, the easier that Bible reading and prophecy will become. Tongues increases your vocabulary, both in the languages of Heaven and in English. Tongues connects you very quickly with the Holy Spirit.

Paul sets a high standard for us by saying, *"I thank God that I speak in tongues more than all of you"* (1 Cor. 14:18). This verse indicates to us that he led a lifestyle of perpetual closeness with the Holy Spirit.

ACTIVATION

If we are baptized in the Holy Spirit then there should be a continual freshness that flows through our lives. We should not only be speaking in the one heavenly tongue but also enjoying the depths of the *fullness* of the gift of tongues.

Ask God to release a new tongue to you right now and speak out loud the freshness of the new language that Holy Spirit gives you.

GOOD PROPHECY: MAINTAINS RELATIONSHIPS

Most of us are only willing to call 5 percent of our present information into question at any one point—that is on a very good day.[26]

—**Ken Wilber, American Psychologist**

Prophetic people turn up in a church or in front of a person and they immediately know that there is *way* more than 5 percent of the belief system looking dodgy; they are *way off* their godly alignment! So how do we navigate the reality that people change slowly? People tend to review their lives in small increments and rarely are they able to handle a wholescale change, even when the prophetic person knows that it is *really* needed.

First, sometimes we *do* have to speak out because God demands it and He wants a wholescale change. But more often we have to *care* about whether the people are ready to hear it. We can save ourselves (and those we prophecy over) a lot of distress by knowing when, where, to whom, and how we best talk about spiritually challenging things.

What this then demands is prophetic people who are faithful and who turn up frequently to stretch others a little bit at a time. We do not want to be messy prophetic types who turn up, spill our guts, leave chaos, and then are never seen again or are never invited to speak into a person's life again.

I believe that around 40 percent of a prophetic person's ministry work is done on a platform giving words or prophesying over an individual in private. However, 60 percent of their work is done *off platform* in relationship building, taking the time to eat together, be together, and becoming a person others can trust to make a withdrawal from.

> **We need to know when, where, to whom, and how we best talk about spiritually challenging things.**

God offers the spirit of wisdom *and* revelation. Stay faithful to relationships and balance this with faithfulness to the voice of God. It's not one or the other; it is both that we are to be mindful of.

Many church leaders are shepherds rather than apostles or prophets. This tends to mean they are low risk in nature, and they exist to keep their people safe. As a prophetic person you will tend to be "higher risk" and have a preference for fast-moving decision-making. Prophetic warriors speak with an intensity because of what they have seen or heard. Revelation immediately impresses on their emotions and they feel it deeply.

This is why you never hear a prophetic warrior speak in shades of gray; it's nearly always black or white. When you have beheld the glory of God or heard Him speak, *you dare not dilute it.* They are never content with the status quo: they rock the boat and nag us until we pay attention to the aspects of our lives that don't reflect God.

Always be mindful that you are wired differently from others by the design of God, and though your words will be challenging, make sure that you are faithful and safe relationally. Prophetic people *must* thrive in church. We are dangerous when we are alone because we become untempered and unsharpened.

> *Prophetic warriors speak with an intensity because of what they have seen or heard.*

May God give you grace to fix any relationships that are broken and maintain relationships with ease.

GOOD PROPHECY: SOMETIMES STAYS SILENT

I recall being utterly shocked when God took me into a season where He asked me to *withhold prophecy.* It was a time of learning to walk away and seeing the things that prophecy cannot ever do. We must know when prophecy is and is not the appropriate tool.

Jesus, in perhaps one of His most frank-sounding statements said, *"Do not give dogs what is sacred; do not throw your pearls to pigs. If you do, they may trample them under their feet, and turn and tear you to pieces"*

(Matt. 7:6). We can get trampled and torn to pieces because we speak too soon, too much, and in the wrong contexts.

> *The spirits of prophets are subject to the control of prophets* (1 Corinthians 14:32).

My words are subject to my will. Just because I see something doesn't mean that I need to share it. What I have seen or heard is subject to my will.

Over the years many of the women who have booked prophetic checkup appointments with us have been sexually abused. One that I remember vividly had come with her new husband. You could see in the spirit her fear of intimacy and the issues that this was creating between them and the problems on the lining of her womb that had led to her current inability to conceive.

Part of them wanted me to spot these issues and another part of them did not. So, I got them to hold hands and close their eyes and I whispered in Jesus's name that, "Fear is coming off the womb," and then I blessed their intimacy. At best, this is only ever a temporary "holding" word. What they really needed was a good pastor and deeper healer to walk them out of where they were. They needed marriage "top tips" and another married couple alongside them. Prophecy was not the tool they needed.

Prophecy is not our central pivot by which all other things spin around.

- Our central pivot is the Word of God and the person of Jesus Christ.

So, in the raising of you to a higher level of prophecy, you must know what it does and what it does not do.

What I have seen or heard is subject to my will.

There is one area that I totally refuse to prophesy into, and it is, "Should I marry this person?" To prophesy into this robs people of the necessary process of choosing to love. Good marriage is a choice that you make every single day, and the Bible tells you what sort of person you should marry in terms of godly character. Marriage choices come in conversations with leaders, when you see if you can live with another's strengths and weaknesses. You need to hear God for yourself with an inner confirmation that this is "the one." Prophecy in this situation robs people of their need to risk their hearts and makes it all too clinical.

GOOD PROPHECY: DOESN'T MIX UP PRAYER AND PROPHECY

When you love someone, you want the best for them. You pray strident prayers in their hearing. You long to deliver a solution in their lives.

If one of your friends is desperately in need of new house, a great prayer to pray is: "God, *would You* give them an amazing house to live in. *Would You* give it to them at a great price and with a really good mortgage deal? *Would You* make it a place that rich memories can be made?" Everyone feels the love that comes from this prayer.

Don't turn a prayer into a prophecy and say, "God is going to give you a house, and He is going to shake the bank to release to you an unheard-of deal in the next few months…." It sounds wonderful, but you are walking that person into major disappointment and problems with prophetic people and problems with God—all because you prophesied what should have been a prayer.

GOOD PROPHECY: HAVE RELATIONSHIPS THAT KEEP PROPHETIC PEOPLE SAFE

Prophecy is not an individual sport.

Get some people around you who cheer you on and weigh what you say.

A culture of teams of people who prophesy is the biblical safeguard for the handling of revelation. Even in the Old Testament you rarely find a prophet alone (they just tend to be a bit dramatic and think they are all alone). Any research into the biblical timeline shows prophets always overlapping in when they prophesy. For example:

- Samuel, Nathan, and Gad are during the reign of King David.
- Samuel has a school of the prophets in three regions, as does Elijah.
- Haggai, Zechariah, and Joel operate in the same time frame.
- Elijah has Elisha.
- Elisha has Gehazi.
- Elisha proves he has Elijah's mantle in front of a "company of prophets."
- Zephaniah, Jeremiah, Obadiah, and Ezekiel overlap.

If there is no wise or capable authority able to protect and validate the prophetic, most prophetic people will get torn to pieces. Find a leader who understands prophecy and stay there.

> *Two or three prophets should speak, and the others should weigh carefully what is said* (1 Corinthians 14:29).

Never get caught alone as a prophetic warrior. Pull yourself out of your cave if you have too. Your extreme black-and-white nature needs to be tempered.

A culture of teams of people who prophesy is the biblical safeguard for the handling of revelation.

THE PROPHETIC WARRIOR

Please give me grace for this next story; this was my reality!

For years as a pharmaceutical sales rep I sold in the cardiology and oncology therapy areas, which all involved fairly sober conversations.

Then, for a while, I moved on to sell Viagra and Movicol (Mira-LAX), and for months all I spoke about in my work life was erectile dysfunction and the shape that correct poo needed to look like! This required bold conversations and the removal of all embarrassment and salaciousness. It all became very matter of fact.

I would fall on my knees, just as I had done since the age of seventeen, and pray a well-rehearsed prayer of decades: "God, why can I not be quieter, more subtle, more tame, more respectable, and less ridiculous? *All* the Christians that I know are and they are more holy. They seem so demure, sophisticated, measured. I just seem to be full-on and both feet first."

I wept my way through years of regret at the extremes in me. Why could I not just tone it down?

Then, one time, my friends at Healing Rooms took a healing team and booked a stall in a New Age psychic fair. All my "proper," holy Christians friends were there with me. And the witches came, and the warlocks stood and eyed us up; they would throw curses and glare intimidatingly and no one seemed to want to be healed.

They did, however, want to know if we knew what God said. At this the rest of the team huddled behind the stall, trying to look as small as they could.

In that moment, my extrovert friend and I got up and we took ourselves out to right in front of our stall. Bravery rose and a courage to speak came. I prayed inwardly, "God, You have trained me in talking professionally about people's private parts, surely I can talk about *You* and put Your words in their ears."

For months in the arena of the psychic fair, right in the midst of the darkness, I understood that God had put in His prophetic people both a love for dealing with difficult things and the bold personalities to handle wickedness. I learned that the prophetic function in the Body of Christ was unique, strange, and wired for bold truth-telling. I received more healing there in that place than almost anywhere else, and eventually from out of those experiences Glasgow Prophetic Centre and the Global Prophetic Alliance were birthed.

God gives prophetic warriors the temperament and personality that can carry revelation. If everyone likes a prophetic warrior, then they are probably doing something wrong.

And so, I joyfully and wholeheartedly release a blessing over you from my home in Glasgow, Scotland, that you might find your extreme, undiluted passion for Jesus and that from this day any cap you have put on your life would be blown off! And that you might dive into the deep oceans of revelation that Jesus has for you–seeing, tasting, feeling, hearing all God has for you.

Where you have dumbed-down your anointing and call, let it be returned to its God-ordained shape! I bless you to know your God and do mighty exploits in His name. I bless you to know, fully, this joyous, wild adventure that is stewarding revelation. I welcome you into the worldwide community of prophetic voices, whose call is to hear God and to shift the status quo, for the sake of the name of Jesus Christ.

Endnotes

INTRODUCTION

1   According to the New American Standard (NAS) Exhaustive Concordance, *megas* (G3173) is used to mean "abundant" once, once as "completely," and once as "surprising," Bible Hub, accessed January 31, 2020, https://biblehub.com/str/greek/3173.htm.

2   As quoted in Dr. Michael Brown, "Who Changed Things?" Charisma Media, February 17, 2014, https://www.charismanews.com/opinion/in-the-line-of-fire/42808-who-changed-things.

CHAPTER 1

3   For example, you can read amazing descriptions of Heaven and the throne room in Ezekiel chapter 1 and 47; Exodus chapter 24; and Revelation chapters 4, 5, 21, and 22.

4   Ezekiel 47:12

5   *"Worthy is the Lamb, who was slain, to receive power and wealth and wisdom and strength and honor and glory and praise!"* (Revelation 5:12).

6　According to Bill Wenstrom, the Hebrew word *chesedh* is often rendered *charis* in Greek. According to Wenstrom, R. Laird Harrison, discussing *chesedh* in the *Theological Wordbook of the Old Testament,* quotes Sidney Hills and Katherine D. Sakenfeld as writing, "*Chesedh* denotes free acts of rescue or deliverance…" (Wenstrom Bible Ministries, accessed February 3, 2020, https://www.wenstrom.org/downloads/written/word_studies/greek/charis.pdf).

CHAPTER 3

7　*"I am the good shepherd; I know my sheep and my sheep know me…. My sheep listen to my voice; I know them, and they follow me"* (John 10:14, 27).

CHAPTER 4

8　Smith Wigglesworth, *Smith Wigglesworth on Faith* (New Kensington, PA: Whitaker House, 1998).

9　I first heard Kathy Walters decree something similar to the foundations of this remarkable set of biblical statements around a decade ago. I've preached it out many, many times since, and so the phraseology may have changed and no doubt I've added to it in places as I've gone along. Thank you, Kathy!

10　"What comes into our minds when we think about God is the most important thing about us. The history of mankind will probably show that no people has ever risen above its religion, and man's spiritual history will positively demonstrate that no religion has ever been greater than its idea of God. Worship is pure or base as the worshiper entertains high or low thoughts of God.

"For this reason the gravest question before the Church is always God Himself, and the most portentous fact about any man is not what he at a given time may say or do, but what he in his deep heart conceives God to be like. We tend by a secret law of the soul to move toward our mental image of God. This is true not only of the individual Christian, but of the company of Christians that composes the Church. Always the most revealing thing about the Church is her idea of God." A.W. Tozer, *The Knowledge of the Holy* (New York: HarperOne, 1961), 1.

11 Jackie Pullinger with Andrew Quicke, *Chasing the Dragon* (London: Hodder & Stoughton, 2006).

12 David Pytches, *Come Holy Spirit: Learning How to Minister in Power* (London: Hodder Christian, 1985), 109.

CHAPTER 5

13 Tomi Arayomi, *Eat, Sleep, Prophesy, Repeat* (Windsor: Tomi Arayomi Ministries, 2018).

CHAPTER 6

14 "The assembly of the people, which in Greek cities had the power of final decision in public affairs....The functions of the ecclesia were: a) To take part in legislation....(b) Election

of officials....(c) The banishment of citizens by ostracism....
(d) Judicial functions in certain exceptional cases only....(e) In
legal co-operation with the Senate the ecclesia had the final
decision in all matters affecting the supreme interests of the
State, as war, peace, alliances, treaties, the regulation of the
army and navy, finance, loans, tributes, duties, prohibition
of exports or imports, the introduction of new religious rites
and festivals, the awarding of honours and rewards, and the
conferring of the citizenship." (Harry Thurston Peck, *Harper's
Dictionary of Classical Literature and Antiquities* [New York:
Harper and Brothers Publishers, 1897, 567–566]).

15 I have had the joy to visit Israel on two occasions. It is possible
to visit the site of the Sanctuary of Pan at Caesarea Philippi
(near the spring at the foot of Mount Hermon) and there is
a helpful artist's impression of what the various temples and
grottos would have looked like in Roman times. I recorded
a short video on location at this site, which you can find on
YouTube by searching for "Emma Stark The Gates of Hell
Shall Not Prevail."

CHAPTER 7

16 Billie Jean King (@BillieJeanKing), 2015, "Champions
keep playing until they get it right. @serenawilliams & @
Venuseswilliams showed that in different ways today!," Twitter,
January 26, 2015, 2:43 a.m., https://twitter.com/billiejeanking/
status/559662884993515522?lang=en.

17 Malcolm Gladwell, *Outliers: The Story of Success* (New York:
Little, Brown and Company, 2008).

CHAPTER 9

18 See I. C. Nuel, *Leaving a Legacy* (Bloomington, IN: West Bow Press, 2014), 92.

CHAPTER 10

19 See Jeremiah 1, especially verses 1:11–14.

20 See Second Kings 6:8–22; Gehazi isn't mentioned by name in this passage but we assume that he is the servant being referred to here.

21 *"And afterward, I will pour out my Spirit on all people. Your sons and daughters will prophesy, your old men will dream dreams, your young men will see visions"* (Joel 2:28 and quoted by Peter in Acts 2:17).

22 I call my "hider angel" a Psalm 91 angel because it functions like those described in verses 11–12: *"For he will command his angels concerning you to guard you in all your ways; they will lift you up in their hands, so that you will not strike your foot against a stone."*

CHAPTER 11

23 For example, see Matthew 13:3–8; First Peter 1:23; James 3:18.

24 *"The LORD was with Samuel as he grew up, and he let none of Samuel's words fall to the ground. And all Israel from Dan to Beersheba recognized that Samuel was attested as a prophet of the LORD. The LORD continued to appear at Shiloh, and there he revealed himself to Samuel through his word"* (1 Sam. 3:19–21).

25 As quoted in Bill Johnson, *Strengthen Yourself in the Lord* (Shippensburg, PA: Destiny Image, 2007).

26 As quoted by Richard Rohr, *Falling Upward* (London: SPCK, 2012).

About Emma Stark

Depending on the taxi driver, hairdresser or shoe salesperson who asks her, Emma will either say she is "a prophet who hears from God", "a travelling lecturer in spirituality", "a church pastor" or "a mum of three wonderful children". If they are being particularly irritating she will tell them she is "an exorcist"! The real answer is that she is actually all of the above—and much more!

EMMA STARK is a prophet who operates with authority and authenticity as she ministers and teaches around the world, giving clear and direct prophetic input to leaders, churches and ministries, equipping the body of Christ to better hear from God and to apply His revelation to transform lives, communities, cities and nations.

Together with her husband, David, she leads an international apostolic hub, a global network of prophetic ministers and one of Scotland's fastest growing churches. Emma has oversight over a strategic prayer network that is raising the faith of prayer warriors across the nations and she mentors a large group of emerging prophets who gather regularly in Scotland from all over the world. As one of the most trusted prophetic voices in the British Isles, Emma sits on prophetic roundtables and councils in Scotland, the

UK and Europe and has twice ministered at the Global Prophetic Summit in Dallas, Texas.

Emma and David are the founding directors of *Glasgow Prophetic Centre,* a Kingdom base manned by nearly 100 experienced prophetic ministers. Thousands from around the world travel to their centre in Scotland to hear from God, receive freedom and be trained and activated in prophecy, revelation and spiritual warfare. Emma and her team have given well over 20,000 hours of face-to-face personal prophetic ministry and have sent millions of *Lion Bites* daily prophetic emails to inboxes around the world, strengthening and encouraging the children of God on every continent. The centre's activities range from "Prophetic Check-Up" appointments to a drop-in "Miracle Clinic"; from deliverance ministry and "Intensive Care" inner healing sessions to a house of prayer and worship; from mentoring and coaching schools to prophetic evangelism on the streets and at new age and "psychic" fairs; from major international gatherings to the support and encouragement of local churches in Scotland and beyond.

Born in Northern Ireland into a long family line of church pastors, Emma communicates with clarity, humour and a fearless Celtic boldness! Emma's father, Pastor John, was a local Baptist church pastor for over 40 years and now works alongside Emma and her team as teaching pastor and "in-house theologian". This background has given Emma a deep love for the church and she loves nothing better than to spend time in prayer, worship and the study of Scripture before teaching, preaching and activating believers into their God-destiny.

Over the years, Emma has been a successful corporate business manager, a media spokesperson, a trained counsellor and a student leader. David and Emma have been involved in leading healing ministries at the local and national level for many years and they have apostolic responsibility for a variety of ministries, ministers and Kingdom businesses. They are ordained ministers with Christian International Europe, under the leadership of Dr Sharon Stone, part of the Christian International Ministries Network founded by Bishop Dr Bill Hamon.

David and Emma live in the heart of the historic city of Glasgow with their three remarkable children, Jessica, Peter and Samuel, and their Labrador retriever, Joy.